THE JEWISH TEEN'S SURVIVAL GUIDE

[HONEST ANSWERS FOR TODAY'S TEENS]

A TARGUM PRESS BOOK

THE JEWISH TEEN'S SURVIVAL GUIDE

RABBI DOVID HOCHBERG

First published 2009
Copyright © 2009 by Dovid Hochberg
ISBN 978-1-56871-477-6

Published by:
TARGUM PRESS, INC.
22700 W. Eleven Mile Rd.
Southfield, MI 48034
E-mail: targum@targum.com
Fax: 888-298-9992
www.targum.com

Distributed by:
FELDHEIM PUBLISHERS
208 Airport Executive Park
Nanuet, NY 10954

Printing plates by Frank, Jerusalem
Printed in Israel by Chish

COVER CONCEPT BY SARAH MERMELSTEIN AND RUCHY BARON

*This book is dedicated
to the teenagers
who have shared their stories,
struggles, and successes
with me.*

Thank you for being real.

RABBI NOACH ORLOWEK

ירושלים, יד מנחם אב תשס"ח

I have read, on a flight to Denver, the entire manuscript of Rabbi Dovid Hochberg, *shlita, The Jewish Teen's Survival Guide* and found it to be practical, and coming from a place of deep compassion and uncommon common sense. I also found that his advice consistently resonated with what I have found to be helpful in helping our youth reach within themselves and discover their own inherent goodness and desire to have a spiritual and meaningful life. May you continue to help our youth, growing up in such a confusing and seductive environment, access and appreciate their own goodness and the treasure that they have within themselves and the heritage that is within their grasp.

בברכת הצלחה ברוח ובגשם,

Noach Orlowek

RABBI MOSHE HEINEMANN
6109 Gist Avénue
Baltimore, MD 21215
Tel. (410) 358-9828
Fax. (410) 358-9838

ה היינעמאן
ד ק"ק אגודת ישראל
טימאר
(410) 764-7778
(410) 764-8878

בס"ד

יתי את חיבורו של ידידי הרב דוד ה?כבערג נ"י שבו מברר עניני השקפה
הגה כפי תוה"ק, שהוא דבר נחוץ להורות לנבוכים ולהעומדים ברגל אחד מנד
וברגל אחד מנד האחר, בפרט בזמן הזה שיש כמה וכמה הפוסחים על שתי
סעיפים ונגררים אחר הדיעות הכוזבות הנמצאים אף בחוצותינו ובקרביותינו.
יבור הזה הוא מורה דרך איך לנהוג לנוח את יצר הרע והסכלות שנתפשט
ולס של התועים שסוברים שאין בהם כח לכבוש את יצרם חבל בקושטוך מעט
את דוחה הרבה חושך.
ן חמינא שדבר טוב עשה המחבר בעמו לחזק את דור החדש להיות יהודיים
עניים לתוה"ק ולדברי חז"ל, גם הדור הישן יכולים ליהנות מהחכמה התבונה
נה הנמצאים במאמרים הללו.
באתי עה"ח באחד בשבת לסדר איש צדיק תמים שבעה ועשרים לחדש תשרי שנת
את תכלפים צבע מאות וששים ותשע לבריאת עולם.
ה בהח"ר ברוך גדכליה כ?עצפתת היינעמאן החונ?? מתא ד??טי?מאר

RABBI MOSHE HEINEMANN
109 Gist Avénue
Baltimore, MD 21215
Tel. (410) 358-9828
Fax. (410) 358-9838

משה היינעמאן
אב״ד ק״ק אגודת ישראל
באלטימאר
טל. 764-7778 (410)
פקס 764-8878 (410)

בס״ד

I have reviewed the manuscript of my dear friend Rabbi Dovid Hochberg, in which he explains basic concepts of השקפה and provides life guidance based on our holy Torah. It is critical to guide those who have questions, particularly in today's day and age, where countless people are drawn to follow the illusions of our streets and surroundings.

This book provides direction on how to successfully overcome the יצר הרע, and dispels the popular belief that it is almost impossible to conquer one's base inclinations. A small measure of truth can drive away much darkness.

Therefore, I declare that the author did an excellent thing to strengthen this generation to be Jews true to the Torah and the words of our Sages, and even older generations will benefit from the wisdom and advice that are found in his words.

Shearith Israel Congregation
קייק שארית ישראל
PARK HEIGHTS AND GLEN AVENUES
BALTIMORE, MARYLAND 21215

YAAKOV HOPFER, RABBI
466-3060 Study
358-8281 Residence

ב האפפער
'טימאר, מד.

To a most esteemed friend, Rabbi Dovid Hochberg, נ"י

It is my great pleasure to write words of introduction on behalf of ידידי בן ידידי.
I am very familiar with Reb Dovid's work and we speak with each other on a
regular basis.

Young men and women growing up in the modern society that envelops us today
face major struggles and נסיונות. There is no person, and certainly no community,
that can insulate itself completely. Simply by walking out in the street, a person
faces these struggles and difficulties. Modern society's attitude towards the
purpose of life, the desire to "make it big" financially, infatuation with sexuality
and focusing on oneself to the detriment of others, all contradict the Torah's
השקפה. It is important for our young men and women to have someone with
whom to speak, who can inspire them to face these issues with confidence and a
strong sense of self-worth. Ideally, this should be done by one's parents who, by
explaining the Torah's viewpoint with the love and warmth that only a parent
can, and by example from personal life, are the best teachers. However, practically
speaking, this does not always happen.

Our Reb Dovid has written a book that "talks" to our youngsters with great
understanding of their issues. This book is written with depth and warmth, in a
very lucid and readable style. Reb Dovid has had wonderful success in his
professional practice in our community of Baltimore. This is because he
understands people and issues, listens to people, and feels great empathy for
them. This book is written in the same manner. Through his personal example,
Reb Dovid has brought about a great Kiddush Hashem, and I am confident that
this book will accomplish the same.

Rabbi Yaakov Hopfer

ט' אייר תשס"ח
May 15, 2008

CONTENTS

ACKNOWLEDGMENTS

Thank you HaKadosh Baruch Hu for all that You give and continue to give. I hope this book will give You *nachas*.

To Bassi Gruen, Avigail Sharer, and the editorial staff at Targum Press, thank you for your insightful comments and professionalism. You make things easy.

To my parents, Mr. and Mrs. Moshe and Laya Hochberg, you have taught me by example and continue to do so. I will always look up to you.

To my in-laws, Rabbi and Mrs. Shaul and Chana Broner, your support and encouragement are very special to me. I'm fortunate to be your son-in-law.

To my family: Efi and Sori Hochberg from Chicago, Brachi and Michoel Soltz from Baltimore, Tami and Yitzchok Dvoretz from Har Nof, Sara and Michoel Eisemann from Detroit, and Ahuva Broner from New York, may we continue to create wonderful memories together.

To my incredible children, Eli, Malky, Menachem, and Naftali, I am thrilled to be your Abba. You make me very proud.

To my amazing wife, Michal, thank you for the beautiful life we share. You make it special beyond words.

WHAT THIS
BOOK IS ABOUT

'm going to assume you are a teenager.

I'm also going to assume that you want honest and straight answers to tough questions.

You see, it's no secret that the teenage years can be challenging, and you might be having a tough time. On one hand, you are on top of the world — spending time with your friends, having fun, checking out new experiences, doing your thing, and enjoying every minute of it.

On the other hand, it isn't always easy dealing with school, parents, and other adults who just don't get it. And sometimes your friends don't turn out to be such good friends after all, and there are many times when you are convinced that no one understands how you feel and what you're going through. You have a lot of questions and very few answers. And you're looking for...well, something.

I don't know if you will find it here.

But I can tell you what you definitely won't find here. You won't find useless and purely theoretical information about adolescence and hormonal changes. You won't read unsympathetic and condescending lectures on platonic relationships and peer pressure.

Trust me, you won't catch me preaching to you.

Here is what you *will* find in these pages...

You will read open and frank discussions of some tough problems and questions and what to do about them. You'll come across practical and useful advice from a Jewish perspective on a variety of subjects, from relationships to music, from parents to self-esteem.

These subjects are taken from articles I used to write for an online advice column, and the readers' responses that follow each chapter are actual questions from kids your own age.* You will find straight talk about some of the difficult issues going on in your life right now.

This book does not touch upon everything. Not even close. But it may make your search for some answers a little easier.

Challenge yourself. Try to reach a new level of understanding. And, more importantly, try to find someone in your life from whom you can continue to learn even more.

I would love to hear from you. Please email me at dh@jewish-parenting.org if there is anything on your mind.

Enjoy.

Rabbi Dovid Hochberg

---

*   Names and details have been changed to protect the privacy of those involved. Any similarities are purely coincidental.

SAFETY NET

A while back, there was an anti-drug slogan that was very popular across the country. "Just Say No." It was plastered on posters in the subway stations. It was frequently played on the radio and television. It was all over the place.

"Just Say No."

There are times when living a Jewish lifestyle takes on the feel of that slogan. Did you ever stop to think about the fact that in Judaism, there are a lot more negative commandments than positive ones? We have 365 negative commandments and only 248 positive commandments! We are human beings with emotions, feelings, and desires. Why did G-d create us that way, imbuing us with powerful urges, only to turn around and tell us, "Just Say No?"

It seems like a cruel joke.

Yet, G-d doesn't play cruel jokes. There must be a reason why He set things up this way.

Let's take a moment and fantasize. Pretend that there are no laws. No rules. No rewards and no punishments. As far as G-d is concerned, you can do whatever you want to do. Play around with that idea for a while. Let your imagination go...

It sounds too good to be true, doesn't it? Imagine! A world where you can do whatever you want.

The truth is that this is not only a fantasy. Pick up a magazine or listen to the news. The media is full of stories about people who actually live their lives this way. People who indulge in whatever they choose without holding themselves back at all. People who live in the world that I am asking you to fantasize about.

But here's the strange part. Keep reading and listening to the stories. Their lives are littered with divorce and rehab programs instead of thrills and joys.

Why?

Simple. Play the fantasy out in your mind for a while and you will see the answer.

That pleasurable feeling doesn't last. As the excitement dies down, you are going to start to feel restless. Bored. Kind of like having an endless summer vacation stretching out before you that is just a little too long. You will feel like you are looking for something that you can't find. You will find yourself feeling...well, I guess the best way to describe the feeling is "empty."

You see, what you have just created is a world without boundaries. You just opened up your personal boundaries and let everything and anything in. There are no limits, no lines that you can draw and say, "This is what I will do and this is what I won't do." There is nothing to define who you are.

Where is the private and personal space that you carve out for yourself? It is no wonder that you begin to experience a sense of emptiness; there are no limits to contain anything.

Now, what happens when you create that private place for yourself? What happens when you create walls, rules, and boundaries around yourself and begin to control what goes in and what comes out? What happens when you set limits about what you will and won't do?

You create something that is uniquely yours. You design a private, personal space that belongs only to you...that *is* you...that you control. You decide what actions, feelings, desires, education, work, recreation, music, hobbies, sports, relationships, friends, etc., will be allowed into that space. You sculpt your own unique and rich creation.

Now, let's get back to our original question. Why did G-d create us with desires and emotions only to tell us, "No, you can't do that"?

Simple. If everything was permitted, how do you set limits? How do you create your personal space? In order to say "no," you have to have temptations and desires for things that you can and cannot do. Saying "no" to this and "yes" to that creates those boundaries and walls that define who you are.

There is also another benefit to boundaries. They keep you safe. They protect you from vulnerable moments.

You see, if you have no boundaries, no point at which you say, "Stop! I am controlling myself. I will not cross this line," then the line will keep moving. You keep pushing and pushing and the game gets more and more dangerous. The risks get greater. Initially, you may have "lived on the edge" by racing a bicycle down a steep hill. Now you need to climb a mountain to give you that same thrill. Tomorrow, who knows what you will need to do to feel that rush?

Actually, as Jews, we have it easier than others. G-d has drawn many of the boundaries for us. We have some flexibility within those boundaries, but for the most part, G-d tells us, "Look, I am going to help you. Follow my guidelines and you will not feel empty. You will never have to worry whether or not a limit that you set is helpful. Follow the limits I provide and you will feel fulfilled. You can go to sleep each night knowing that you did the right thing."

And the feeling of knowing you did the right thing makes winning the struggle worth it.

READERS RESPOND

Dear Rabbi,

I like your idea about the risks getting greater. I think it is true that "your line" can keep moving if you don't set a limit. There is only one problem I have with the idea. What if you don't care that the risks are getting greater? When you just say to yourself, it doesn't really matter if I do something very risky. I find myself doing that a lot. What should I do?

Yonah

Dear Yonah,

Well, the first thing I would do is ask myself, "Why don't I care that the risks are getting greater?"

There has got to be an answer to that question.

It might not be an answer that you want to hear, but there is an answer to that question.

That's where I would start. That answer is going to point you in a direction that gets you thinking. For example, perhaps the answer is that you don't really think too highly of yourself, or maybe you believe that nobody cares about you. Those answers may hurt, and may hurt deeply, but those answers are the real reasons you want to do something risky. Not because you don't care about the risk.

It's because you think you are worth risking.

People generally don't risk valuable and precious items, and if they do, they certainly don't take big risks. Valuable items need to be protected.

Do you feel you aren't worth protecting, so it doesn't matter that the risks are getting greater?

Yonah, you are unique and have a unique purpose in this world.

I assure you that you are valuable and worth protecting.

Rabbi Hochberg

Dear Rabbi,

Doesn't it still seem that there are too many "no's" and not enough "yes's?" As Jews, there are so many things we can't do and it gets kind of stifling, if you know what I mean.

I understand your point about needing no's to make yes's special, but don't you think we could accomplish the same thing with fewer no's?

Amy

Dear Amy,

Logically speaking, you are correct. We probably could get away with fewer no's and still create good boundaries. And I understand that it sometimes feels overwhelmingly difficult and stifling.

But there is another part of us that has nothing to do with logic as we know it. Our *neshamah*, our spiritual side, is just as real as our physical body and uses a different form of logic.

It is called spiritual logic, or G-d's will.

Think of it in terms of a physical law like gravity or the speed of light. We may not understand the how's and why's of gravity, but we know that when we drop something, it falls to the ground. Spiritual laws are the same way. We may not see them operate or understand why they operate, but the fact remains that when we do a mitzvah, we accomplish something spiritually. When we give charity or daven, we create tremendous spiritual benefit for our *neshamah*, even if we don't feel or see it.

G-d, in His infinite wisdom, gave us the Torah and all of its commandments. He informed us that when we perform them, we build great spiritual masterpieces. G-d also decided, in His infinite wisdom, that we needed a certain number of no's and certain number of yes's in order to accomplish this task.

This is spiritual logic and every "no" and every "yes" is critically important. We need every single one and can't afford to leave any out... even if we don't understand the reason.

There is also another idea that is important to understand. G-d created and loves each and every one of us. He is fully aware of our struggles and challenges and takes this into consideration every step of the way. He knows that sometimes we will succeed and sometimes we won't.

Our job isn't to be perfect.

Our job is to try.

Rabbi Hochberg

WHY YOU SHOULD
SURRENDER

nspiration strikes at the strangest times.

The idea for this chapter came to me toward the end of a workout this morning. You know, the point when the clock says ten more minutes and you can't last ten more seconds? You know you have to keep going, but ten minutes seems like an eternity. Your arms and legs are aching, your chest is on fire, and your muscles are burning. You are in agony.

How do you get through it?

I'll tell you what worked for me. I told myself, "I can last for one more minute... One more minute and then I'll quit... I'll end early today. Just hang in there for one more minute..."

Well, that got me through the first minute. Although my muscles were really aching now, I repeated my pep talk. "One more minute. It's easy, just one more minute and you can quit. Come on, you can do one more minute..."

It worked again. I completed another minute. And another. And another.

Why did this approach work? I set up a reasonable goal and promised myself a reward. "Only one more minute and then you can quit." Anyone can push himself for one more minute — and the promise of quitting was so tempting. The trick is to break formidable tasks into small pieces and to focus on each piece, one at a time.

Let me give you a powerful way to use this idea. The Talmud (*Sukkah* 52b) tells us that every day the *yetzer hara* tries to destroy a person and, without G-d's help, he would be successful. We are all familiar with the strength and ingenuity that the *yetzer hara* brings to his work. He's very, very good at his job.

But here's how you can beat him at his own game.

Give in to him. Surrender. Indulge yourself. But only indulge yourself after an hour. For example, you just heard some great gossip and are dying to share it with a friend. Tell yourself, "Yes, I have a tremendous desire to share this story with my friends, and I know I shouldn't. But I can't control myself and will definitely wind up telling them today. However, I will do it in an hour, not now." You will suddenly find it easier to fight off the desire. It will feel as though a weight has been lifted from your shoulders.

Why does this technique work? Well, in a sense, it's a mind game (which is a great technique to use when dealing with the *yetzer hara*, the undisputed master of mind games). You are telling yourself that you *will* share the story with your friends. You are just going to wait an hour. The hour will pass relatively easily.

What should you do when the hour is up? You know the drill: "Give me another twenty minutes and I will really go pick up the phone. I mean it. I will totally say whatever I want. In twenty minutes. It's only twenty minutes." When the twenty minutes are up, try to push further. You may not be able to control yourself completely, but look at what you accomplished. You were ready to do the wrong thing immediately. Now, you controlled yourself for an hour and twenty minutes.

Impressive!

This technique does not always work, depending on the strength of your desire for the particular forbidden action. Keep in mind, though, that for every second you avoid doing an *aveirah*, you earn incredible reward. Reward you can't even imagine. And you earn that reward even if you give in at the end.

Play around with this idea. You will discover that it becomes easier and easier to apply. Also, you will find that more and more frequently, events will take place that will prevent you from doing the wrong thing. This is called *siyata diShmaya*, help from Heaven. It is a sign from G-d that you are on your way.

READERS RESPOND

Dear Rabbi,

Does this really work? I mean, if I know that eventually I'm going to give in, what's the point of trying? I can't see myself trying too hard to fight the yetzer hara just to do the wrong thing at the end.

Moshe

Dear Moshe,

I don't know if you will give in at the end. You don't know if you will give in at the end. But I will guarantee you one thing:

If you decide to be strong for a short amount of time, say ten minutes, you will probably not give in until the ten minutes are up. Motivating yourself to decide to be strong for those ten minutes may be extremely difficult, and you might give up before you start. That is where most people get stuck. However, once you're motivated to hang in there for ten minutes, and the ten minutes begin, you are almost guaranteed to be strong for that time.

How many ten-minute time periods can you last? There is no way of knowing the answer. But the point is, it really doesn't matter. Don't focus on the end. Focus on just starting the next ten minutes and you are almost guaranteed success for those ten minutes.

You'll deal with the next ten minutes later.

Rabbi Hochberg

Dear Rabbi,

What if I don't feel like fighting with myself to do the right thing? Sometimes it is too exhausting to fight and I just don't want to do it. I know I shouldn't think this way, but sometimes that is just the way I feel. What should I do in this kind of situation?

Rebecca

Dear Rebecca,

That is a hard question to answer.

You see, there are three kinds of situations. You can (and do) fight, or you simply can't (and don't) fight, or the tricky, third situation where you might be able to fight but it takes so much effort and energy.

It is that third type of situation that is the most frustrating and difficult.

Our mission in this world is to try. And sometimes, even though you try as hard as you can, you don't succeed and you lose the battle. But this is the point: your goal is to win the war, even though you may lose individual battles. So what should you do next time you are faced with a tough situation? Try again.

Life is a marathon, not a sprint.

Rabbi Hochberg

WHY BAD THINGS HAPPEN
TO GOOD PEOPLE

t's the ultimate question. It's the question that has been bothering mankind since the beginning of time. It is the question that we struggle with constantly as we experience the ups and downs of life.

Why do bad things happen to good people?

The Torah (*Shemos* 33, 19–20) tells us that Moshe, our greatest leader, asked G-d an unusual question. Moshe asked G-d if he could see His face. G-d responded that He would show Moshe His back, for no living mortal would be able to see His face (see *Berachos* 7a).

What is this strange discussion about faces and backs and what does it have to do with our question? The answer is that seeing a person's face allows you to recognize him easily. You can pick him out in a crowd or identify him from far away. However, if all you see is a person's back, it will be much more difficult to recognize him later in a crowd. You didn't see him clearly enough.

Moshe asked to see G-d's face. "Please," Moshe asked, "let me see You clearly. Show me how You interact with the world and why You do all the things that You do. I want to see You clearly in all that happens in life, whether it seems good or bad."

G-d responded, "No, Moshe, you cannot see My face. Since you are a mortal, you will not be able to fully comprehend all of My actions. However, I will show you My back and allow you to partially understand why I do certain things. But you will not be able to see Me clearly and understand why I seemingly make good things happen to bad people and bad things happen to good people."

The greatest Jewish leader in history was not given a clear answer to this question. So, you are probably wondering what I am going to tell you...

The truth is that the title of this chapter is misleading. It really should read "What Should We Do When Bad Things Happen to Good People?" You see, we don't know why bad things happen to good people. Yes, there are countless explanations that can answer parts of this question, but no one has the complete answer.

That's the reality of it. The bottom line is that we don't know why.

However, we do have control over our responses and reactions to a tragedy.

Rav Shmuel Yaakov Weinberg, *zt"l*, the former *rosh yeshivah* of Ner Israel Rabbinical College in Baltimore, would always say, "Troubling times require a response."

When something bad happens, you need to respond. You need to react.

It doesn't really matter what the response is; the important thing is that you respond in a positive way.

Let me give you an example: Suppose tragedy strikes, G-d forbid, and someone who you care about suddenly passes away. You are shocked. Confused. Angry. You question why G-d allowed such a terrible thing to happen.

You need to react to this tragedy. You need to respond in some way. Perhaps you will decide to improve a particular character trait. You might choose to be more careful with your speech or perform an extra mitzvah. Maybe you will try to work on an important relationship that has fallen apart over the last few months. You may start giving more charity or helping other people more. Try to improve yourself in some way.

Let me explain why it is helpful to respond in this way. You see, we don't have control over many things in our lives. When tragedy strikes, we feel helpless and angry. We were powerless to stop it. We desperately want to control what happens, but that just isn't the way life works. In fact, that is why we usually ask many questions about a tragedy, trying to understand the minutest detail of what actually happened. The feeling of being out of control is very frightening. On some level, we believe that if we understand exactly what took place, we can control whether or not it will happen again.

However, when we respond in some positive way, we regain a sense of control. The message we are giving ourselves is, "I don't understand why this terrible tragedy happened. I had no control over what happened. But it won't be wasted on me. I do have control over how I react and I will react in a positive way to show that what happened made an impact on me. One thing is certain. This awful misfortune is causing me to take steps to become a better person."

The interesting part is that you will feel better when you react in this manner.

No one knows why bad things happen to good people. But if they do happen, G-d forbid, try to grow from the experience.

READERS RESPOND

Dear Rabbi,

How can a perfect G-d create evil?

Miriam

Dear Miriam,

This concept is extremely complex and probably one of the most difficult questions that people ask. There are several approaches. Here's one of them:

G-d gave people *bechirah*, the freedom of choice, to decide between good and evil. Man receives reward for making the right choices in life. One can only do that if there is evil in existence as well. However, evil isn't inherently bad. It is a tool, just like good, to allow man to make choices and experience the consequences of his choices.

This is a very simplistic approach, but I believe it answers your question.

Rabbi Hochberg

Dear Rabbi,

How can G-d expect perfection from us if humans are not perfect? Why must the righteous get punished for the smallest thing? Can't G-d just say "You've done so much already, and since you're only human, I'll forgive you for the small things?"

Sara

Dear Sara,

G-d does not expect perfection from us. We aren't angels. We were given the ability to do right and wrong and the ability to master the urge to do wrong.

You are asking a very deep question. The answer lies in understanding the spiritual challenges of the righteous. For example, take a school bully who steals other children's lunch money and cruelly spits at them after he takes their money. One time, after a difficult, internal struggle, he holds himself back from spitting at his victim after he steals his money. This bully just fought a battle within him and exercised self-control by not spitting. This bully's struggles are far below the battles that we have. We have other battles. And great, righteous people have battles that are far above our battles.

The point is that every individual struggles and has spiritual battles.

The battles just take place on his or her particular level. It may seem to us that the righteous only committed a tiny infraction, but the reality is that what we are calling a tiny infraction is the equivalent of you losing one of your battles and the bully losing one of his. For the righteous, the stakes are higher, the rewards are greater, and the penalties are more severe.

But it is the same battle.

If we can't understand the severity of the punishment, it is because the battle is taking place far above our understanding. The bully wouldn't understand your battles, to respect your parents or help out a friend, for example. He couldn't comprehend how a person could be punished for such an infraction. It is too far above him. And the challenges of the completely righteous are far above our challenges.

I hope that was helpful. It is a very deep concept.

Rabbi Hochberg

Dear Rabbi,

Thank you for your answer. I still have a question, though. Isn't G-d demanding perfection from us by expecting us to win every battle?

Sara

Dear Sara,

G-d always provides us with the opportunity to win. We can always choose to respond to any challenge in the best possible way, even if it means choosing between two very difficult options. However, that doesn't mean that we will always win or make the best choice. But we always have to try.

People are not perfect and succumb to the *yetzer hara*. G-d created us, and, believe me, He knows this and takes it into consideration when presenting us with challenges.

Also, sometimes we think we understand what the challenge is supposed to be, but we are really mistaken. The real challenge might be something easier than we think. For example, if someone is fighting with her parents about curfew, the actual challenge (for that person's particular level) might be not to yell when she is angry. However, she might think that the challenge is not to feel angry at all. If she can't do that, she will get frustrated and angry at herself for failing a test that she isn't even supposed to be taking.

Our mission in life is to try. No more and no less.

Rabbi Hochberg

Dear Rabbi,

I really enjoy reading your articles because they deal with practical concepts. I once read that there are only nine inches that separate a person from accomplishing his goals in life. Most people have a good deal of knowledge stored in their head. All they have to do is move the knowledge nine inches from their heads into their hearts. Your chapters help me take the knowledge from my head and apply them in my heart. Thank you so much!

I have a question.

I understand that G-d can punish a person through someone else. For example, the Egyptians enslaved the Jews and the Romans destroyed the Beis HaMikdash. Obviously, the Jews deserved these tragedies, and these nations were merely the conduits through which G-d punished the Jews. I am having a very hard time with this concept. If G-d wants someone to get punished, and He gives the idea to another person to inflict pain upon him, why is the one who inflicts the pain held accountable?

I really don't understand this idea.

Aviva

Dear Aviva,

There are several answers to this question and I will share one of them with you. We find the concept that G-d uses good people to do good things and evil people to do evil things. It is true that the Jews were supposed to be enslaved in Egypt. In fact, G-d told this to our forefather

Avraham hundreds of years earlier. Yet, simply because G-d knew this to be the future, this did not take away the choice of the Egyptians to act cruelly. They made the choice to be evil, so they were used as tools to fulfill the destiny of the Jewish nation.

You see, when G-d decides that a person needs to be punished, the means and ways through which he will be punished are determined by the level of righteousness of the "inflictor." If the potential inflictor is a righteous person, G-d will not use him to punish someone else. If he is an evil person, he will be used to punish others in order that he will receive more retribution for his misdeeds.

This idea is expressed by the great sage Hillel in *Pirkei Avos* (2:7), when he saw a skull floating on the water and said, "Since you drowned others, you were drowned, and the ones who drowned you, will be drowned."

At the very least, it is certainly an incentive to be a good person!

Rabbi Hochberg

Dear Rabbi,

Aharon, the kohen gadol, didn't do anything when his sons were killed (see Vayikra 10:1–7), which included not showing any signs of mourning. Was he allowed to react in the positive manner that you described in your article or not? If he did react, what middah or mitzvah did he take on or improve upon?

Aliza

Dear Aliza,

Aharon was praised for controlling himself in accepting the decree of G-d silently. However, the Torah does not tell us what, if anything, he did as a result of the decree. The point I was making in the essay is that we need to respond to a tragedy in some positive way. I was not discussing the way we should accept a tragedy.

The best acceptance is silent acknowledgment and faith in G-d's will. The best response is positive action.

Rabbi Hochberg

Dear Rabbi,

I know a girl who is having a lot of trouble believing in G-d because her grandfather was killed in the Holocaust. She denies that there is a G-d or that He is involved in the world. I tried to speak with her and explain that G-d has a plan for everyone, but she doesn't want to accept anything I say. For example, she asked me how I can say there is a G-d when He allowed a Holocaust to happen?

What can I tell her?

Zahava

Dear Zahava,

This is a very difficult issue. The bottom line is that we don't understand why the Holocaust happened and why her grandfather was killed.

First and foremost, I would empathize with her as much as possible. Her family went through a horrific experience and she is still struggling with the pain. Try to understand how difficult it must have been for her and her family.

Second, I would tell her that there is a level of maturity at which we accept things as real even though we can't see or understand them. For example, we don't necessarily understand how gravity works or how light travels, but we accept their existence as reality. The same idea applies here. We don't know why G-d did what He did. We are angry at G-d for doing what He did. We wish it never happened. But all these thoughts don't take away the reality that G-d exists.

We don't understand. But we accept.

A small child does not believe something is real unless he can actually see it. As we get older, we accept more and more as reality even though we can't explain it.

Belief in G-d is the same idea. It is belief, no question about it. As the expression goes, "The believers have no questions and the non-believers have no answers." Even with all the proofs in the world, the bottom line is that a person has to *want* to believe. Accepting that there is a G-d even though we are angry at what He has done is not contradictory at all.

Remember, you aren't trying to convince her that everything G-d does is for the good. That comes later. Your goal now is to convince her that G-d exists even if we don't understand all that He does.

Good luck. Let me know what happens.

Rabbi Hochberg

Dear Rabbi,

I think, with all due respect, that the basic premise that you suggested for this article is not correct. You should be telling people that everything G-d does is good and that there is no bad. Don't you agree?

Avraham

Dear Avraham,

You are 100% correct. Everything that comes from G-d is good. Fortunate is the individual who achieves this level of understanding and acceptance.

However, most people out there are not yet able to internalize this level of acceptance. Telling them "All is for the good" sounds patronizing and fake. It makes them think, "That's easy for you to say. I bet if you were in my position, you would think otherwise."

And maybe they're right.

In fact, there are events that we are told by the ancient Rabbis to perceive as "bad" and deal with accordingly.

The purpose of this article was to give people a practical way to deal with difficult times. Obviously, the ideal way would be to internalize the idea that you mentioned. But the vast majority who cannot, can use the practical method outlined in the chapter as an alternative way of dealing with tragedy.

Rabbi Hochberg

Dear Rabbi,

Why do we react to a tragedy, such as a death, by working harder to do a mitzvah or by improving a middah? If the death does not relate to me at all, why should I be the one working?

Rachelle

Dear Rachelle,

In the article, I was referring to situations where people may feel helpless when a tragedy strikes. Usually that happens when the tragedy affects them or someone they are close with. However, people are also affected when they hear about something terrible, G-d forbid, that happens to someone they don't even know.

However, even if you think that person's death does not relate to you, nothing happens without a reason. Why did G-d cause you to hear about a particular tragedy? There is a reason for that. We don't always know the reason, but there is a reason. We don't have control over what happened, but we do have control over how we respond.

On a deeper level, all Jews are connected. Something negative — and certainly something positive — that happens to a Jew is somehow related to all of us. This is a very complex concept. We can discuss this further if you would like.

Rabbi Hochberg

Dear Rabbi,

A girl in my class lost her father last month. Some of the girls were saying that they were taking on extra mitzvos in his zechus. I did not know how I should react to his death. Should I do something in his memory?

Shira

Dear Shira,

Anything we do in the *zechus* of someone who passed away has an unbelievable impact on the person's *neshamah*. In certain instances, it can even elevate him from Gehinom to Gan Eden (see *Midrash Tanchuma*, beginning of *parashas Ha'azinu*). If you decide to take on a particular mitzvah in his memory, it is an act of great *chesed,* and you should be very proud of yourself.

Kindness shown toward someone who passed away is referred to as "*chesed shel emes*," because there is no way for the recipient to ever repay the favor.

May G-d reward you for your kindness and sensitivity.

Rabbi Hochberg

ATTRACTION AND DESIRE

D esire. Attraction. Relationships. Powerful emotions.

Do I have your attention yet?

I would like to explore with you the Jewish perspective on desire and attraction between the genders on a practical and emotional level. First, I'll introduce two concepts that are essential for you to understand before the real discussion begins. Second, I'll present four very important ideas that hopefully will help you understand and relate personally to the Jewish perspective.

Here are the two concepts:

In His infinite wisdom, G-d created an extremely powerful attraction between the genders. It exists, and cannot be ignored. The Rabbis explain that G-d did this in order to perpetuate the human race. Without desire and attraction, people would not reproduce and the world would remain desolate.

Unlike some other religions, Judaism strongly encourages marriage. In fact, the first mitzvah in the Torah commands us to have children. The

Torah recognizes this attraction as being very real. The message is simple. We must acknowledge and accept these powerful emotions between the genders in order to learn how to deal with them properly.

The second concept is that, contrary to what you might believe, you do have control over your actions and behavior. You don't always have control over your thoughts and desires — that's a separate issue — but you do have control over your response to those thoughts and desires. I know that some of you may disagree with me now. You believe that it is impossible not to act on your thoughts. While you are correct that it can be extraordinarily difficult, I will show you that you do have control.

The Talmud (*Avodah Zarah* 17a) relates a fascinating story. There was a man named Elazar ben Dordaya who indulged himself completely in immoral behavior. One time, he was told by an immoral woman that his ways would lead him to Gehinom. After some thought, he decided to repent. He went to the mountains and asked them to pray for him. The mountains responded, "We have to pray for ourselves." He asked the sky, the earth, the sun, the moon, and the stars to pray for him, and they all responded the same way, "We have to pray for ourselves."

Why was Elazar asking the mountains, the sky, and the moon to pray for him? What was he thinking?

I believe this is what he was trying to accomplish. He thought that by going to the mountains and the stars, he was making an important point. He was saying, "Mountains, you are part of the natural order of the world, and I am part of the natural order of the world. G-d created you, and G-d created me. You have no control over yourselves, and I have no control over my desires. It is not my fault. Pray for me that I should be forgiven, because you and I are equal when it comes to having no control over our actions."

The mountains responded, "Even though we are only mountains, we still have to pray. The fact that we have no control over our physical existence doesn't eliminate our need to connect to G-d. You are a human being, a creature with control over his desires and behavior. You certainly have to pray, repent your misdeeds, and act appropriately.

Don't blame G-d for what you have done. Deal with your behavior and its consequences."

After repeating this conversation with the sky, the earth, the sun, etc., the significance of what he was hearing sunk into Elazar. It dawned on him that he could not blame his actions on the way he was created. He would have to make choices, act appropriately, and repent if he wanted forgiveness.

And so, he began to pray.

Keep these two concepts (acknowledging the attraction between men and women and realizing that we do have control over our actions) in mind as we begin to examine the Jewish perspective on relationships.

What exactly is the Jewish perspective on relationships? Specifically, what is the Jewish view on dating and everything that goes along with it? What is the point of *tzenius, yichud,* and *shemiras negiah*? Are we really expected to keep all of it? All the time?

Let's begin with the first idea...

1. SELF-CONTROL

The first two human beings, Adam and Chavah, were given one mitzvah to observe: don't eat from the *eitz hada'as*, the Tree of Knowledge. After they ate from the tree, they realized that they were naked and became embarrassed.

What changed?

One of the answers given (see commentary of the Rosh and the *Derashos Beis HaLevi)* is that Adam and Chavah realized that there was nothing inherently special in the fruit of the *eitz hada'as*. It didn't taste any differently from the other fruits. It didn't look any differently from the other fruits. The *only* difference was that they were commanded not to eat it. "Don't eat it," G-d said, "because I told you not to eat it. Not for any other reason. Obeying me, practicing self-control, is what makes the fruit of this tree special."

After they ate from the tree, after they realized that the fruit itself was not what was special, they saw this point clearly. The holiness and power of the *eitz hada'as* came simply from the control they had exercised over their behavior (before they ate from it). When they didn't exercise that self-control, all of a sudden, their physical needs and desires were no longer special. They immediately became ashamed of their physical desires. Self-control, obeying G-d's will, is the *only* thing that turns natural and normal physical behavior into something pure and special.

Self-control is what makes relationships special.

Self-control is what separates a sublime relationship from one rooted only in physical desire. This is a complicated idea, but let me sum it up in one sentence: It is your ability to say "no" that makes your "yes" so incredibly special. If you are free with your actions and don't deny yourself any pleasure, what makes your actions special? It is only when you control yourself and limit your actions that they have meaning. Not doing, not giving in to temptations, is what makes your life richer.

You can't experience the wonderful feeling of a "yes" if you have never experienced a "no."

Yes, it is hard. Yes, it is very difficult to do. You're right. And G-d knows that. He created us with powerful physical desires. He also provided us with a framework for relationships between the genders. It's called marriage. This relationship has the potential to be incredibly special. Marriage allows a man and a woman, together with G-d, to create life. A husband and wife become partners with G-d in Creation, so to speak.

The Talmud has many expressions that strongly encourage marriage. For example, "One who lives without a wife, lives without happiness, without blessing, and without goodness" (*Yevamos* 62b). The Torah itself tells us, "It is not good for man to be alone, I will create a helper for him" (*Bereishis* 2:18). The union of man and woman is necessary for the two of them to fulfill their individual and combined potential.

Remember, when you are finally able to say yes within the framework that the Torah provides, it will truly be special *because* you have said no.

Which brings us to our second idea...

2. BOUNDARIES

Have you ever wondered why the rich and famous of Hollywood seem to have it all, yet so many of them wind up involved in divorce, drugs, and immoral behavior? What drives these people to the edge of what we would call "normal" behavior? And who thought up bungee jumping? Or why would people play Russian roulette with a loaded gun? Why turn pleasure into pain? What drives thinking people to push their limits to the point of risking death?

The answer is simple. Lack of boundaries. If you have no boundaries, then when do you stop? Where do you stop? And perhaps the most important question, why should you stop?

When it comes to relationships between men and women, the Torah and the Rabbis established guidelines and boundaries. We don't even need to come up with boundaries on our own; they have already done that for us. The boundaries are so brilliant, so intuitive, and they reflect deep insight into human nature. The boundaries protect the self-respect and emotions of both sides and keep them from vulnerable moments when they may act in a way they will regret later.

Let's take *yichud* as an example.

The law of *yichud* is that one may not be alone with a member of the opposite gender who is not a spouse, mother, daughter, or sister. It doesn't matter if you are alone together because you are working on a project. It doesn't matter if you are alone together because you just happen to find yourselves alone. The law is clear on this issue: do not be alone together. At first glance, it seems a bit extreme. You are not allowed to be alone together? What do you think is going to happen already? Come on, you have your limits.

Let's move away from the religious perspective for a minute and analyze this from a purely psychological and emotional perspective.

You may like her. She may like you. Obviously, both of you have lines that you will not cross when it comes to inappropriate behavior. You have self-respect and know that you will keep to those guidelines. You know that you would not be able to look at yourself in the mirror the next day if you crossed your line, wherever that particular line may be. There is nothing to be concerned about.

Now, all of a sudden, you find yourself alone with her. You glance at each other. The attraction and desire is there. No one is around and no one will know. Everyone has a vulnerable moment. What will you do? Will you cross your line? How far? What will it feel like, knowing that your line, your boundary that you always said you wouldn't cross, has just been violated?

I know some of you will say, I am stronger than that. I will never cross my line, no matter what. That may be true, but let me ask you something. What requires greater effort: controlling yourself when you are never alone together or controlling yourself when you are alone in a room with him or her and the attraction is there?

The law of *yichud* provides you with a boundary that does not require superhuman self-control on your part. It protects you from moments of vulnerability, when you may do something that you feel bad about later. You must admit that it is a lot more difficult to control yourself from acting inappropriately when you are alone together than when you are not. Don't put yourself in that position. Don't play near the edge of a cliff. True, nothing may happen, but why take the risk? Don't forget, you have to look yourself in the mirror tomorrow.

Make it easy on yourself.

The same is true of the other laws surrounding relationships. *Tzenius* is another example. The Torah is not being harshly restrictive about what you can and cannot wear, say, and act. It is providing you with the boundaries necessary for you to feel good about yourself and enjoy healthy self-respect and self-esteem. Of course, you want to dress and act a certain way. That's normal. The desire and attraction are there, no question about it. The Torah is giving you an easy way to maintain your boundaries. An easy way to make sure that the lines you really don't want to cross won't be violated, and a way for you to feel special without needing the approval of someone else. Dress, speak, and act modestly and you won't need to fight with yourself and run the risk of crossing your line. Like I said earlier, it is simply safer not to play near the edge of the cliff.

The same applies for *shemiras negiah*. It's not about what you aren't allowed to do. It's about providing you with strong boundaries. Think about it. The Torah is protecting you from fighting with one of your most powerful desires. Don't touch each other at all. Now, you don't have to worry about being intimate up to a certain point and then stopping. Stopping in the "heat of the moment" takes incredible self-control, control that is difficult for most of us. Even if you can control yourself, why risk it? Simply follow the Torah's guidelines and life suddenly gets a lot less stressful.

Boundaries, boundaries...it's all about boundaries. Respect them. (See chapter "Safety Net" for more discussion on the topic of boundaries.)

Which brings us to the third idea...

3. FEELING GOOD

Tell me the truth. Have you ever felt bad after you did the right thing? I don't mean upset about missing out on whatever else you could have been doing. I am not asking if you were angry and frustrated at the time. You probably were. I'm talking about a situation where you were confronted with making a choice, a decision, to either do the right thing or the wrong thing, and you decided to do the right thing. How did you feel looking back at your choice? Did you feel good about yourself or not?

I am willing to bet that when you looked back and reflected on your decision, you felt good. You felt accomplished. You felt like you were in control. And guess what? You did just demonstrate that you actually were in control.

It is a basic fact of life: People feel good about themselves when they make the right choices and do the right thing. In fact, the more desperately you want to do the wrong thing, the better you will feel about yourself if you decide not to do it.

Here's an example. A girl or guy asks you if you would like to spend some time with her or him alone. Alone in a manner that you know is not permissible. You know it is the wrong thing to do. But, come on! Just one time! You really like him or her and you just want to talk privately. But you know it's wrong. But you want so desperately to talk! You struggle with the conflicting thoughts in your mind.

What should you do?

You will have to make that decision. However, let me tell you what you will feel like if you decide to do the right thing and say no. You will feel accomplished and in control. Your self-esteem will soar because you just proved to yourself that *you* are in charge of your life, and although you can say yes, you also know how to say no. Think about that feeling. Is it worth it? That is up to you. You are the one who will have to live with your decision. All I am asking you to do is to think long and hard about how you will feel if you do the wrong thing and how you will feel if you do the right thing.

Which brings us to the fourth idea...

4. SPIRITUAL AND PHYSICAL REWARD

I'm not even going to get into describing the reward that awaits you in the Next World for controlling your desires. We don't have any comprehension of how great it is. Instead, I would like to share a thought with you about the reward you can receive in this world.

Rabbi Nachman of Breslov would often quote a *Zohar* that controlling one's desires creates the channel for *berachah*, abundance and success, to flow into the world. Practically, what that means is that if you control yourself, G-d will cause *berachah* to flow into all that you do. You will begin to accomplish more, to become more successful. You will begin to see an extra measure of *siyata diShmaya*, help from Heaven, in all of your actions.

Remember, there is a tremendous amount of spiritual energy out there that G-d is waiting to give to us as long as we try.

READERS RESPOND

Dear Rabbi,

I need to ask you a question. I have a boyfriend for three months now and I know it is almost impossible to control your emotions with the opposite sex (especially if you are a teenager). The problem is that as the years go by, I have stronger and stronger feelings for men. I know I should be shomer negiah, but the truth is that I am not so careful. (He isn't shomer at all.)

Is it okay if I am not shomer, or should I be shomer from a common-sense perspective? Will G-d forgive me if I repent later for not being shomer? I need help. I need to talk to a rabbi that I can be open with and discuss my problems. I am looking for advice from a realistic point of view instead of a religious point of view. Sort of like advice from one friend to another friend. Please help me!

Tamar

Dear Tamar,

It is normal for your feelings toward men to get stronger as time passes. The good news is that you also get a stronger sense of maturity and control as you get older. I understand that it isn't easy, though.

G-d always forgives you if you repent. There is no question about that. (Although, if a person sins planning to repent, G-d may make the process of repenting more difficult.) But I have a question for you. What is going to make you repent later that won't make you repent now? What do you think is going to change in the future? What will be different?

You asked me to respond from a realistic point of view (not a religious point of view), from a friend's perspective, and I will. You want to know if you could have a relationship with your boyfriend and not be *shomer negiah*.

Here's my answer:

You shouldn't have such a relationship because it cheapens you and can ultimately make both you and your boyfriend lose respect for each other. Let's be honest: A physical relationship with your boyfriend is less about you and him as people and more about the way it makes both of you feel. It obscures your unique qualities and talents, the parts of you that are really special. So tell me...is that really what you want for both of you?

You also shouldn't because you are a Jewish girl and that makes you special. Automatically. Whether you are religious or not, you come from a pretty impressive lineage. You are distinctive and valued, and distinctive people act in a certain way.

You are very confused now. I understand that. You want your boyfriend to continue his relationship with you. Yet, you want to do the right thing. You want to be able to respect yourself. It is so confusing, it is driving you crazy.

Here's my advice to you. Do the right thing. Don't think about it. Don't analyze how it feels. Just do it. Tell him no. It will be very difficult to do at first; I certainly don't expect your feelings for your boyfriend to just fade away. But it will get easier as time goes on.

You are more special than you realize. Give yourself the respect that you deserve.

Rabbi Hochberg

Dear Rabbi,

    A few weeks ago, I discovered that someone in my house has been looking at extremely inappropriate pictures and websites on the Internet. I know that it must be my older brother (who is 20), since he is the only one besides me who uses the computer. He is very careful to delete all the evidence when he is done looking at the Web sites, but sometimes he isn't careful enough. That is how I discovered it in the first place.

I don't know what to do. I can't confront my brother without destroying our relationship. I can't tell my parents for fear of causing them pain. I want my brother to understand the spiritual danger of looking at the Web sites and pictures. He probably doesn't realize that what he is doing is wrong. I have tried dropping small hints, but I really am at a loss about what to do.

Ari

Dear Ari,

You are in a difficult situation, and I commend you for trying to help your brother.

You mentioned that talking to your brother about the websites would destroy your relationship with him. Why do you think so? What is your relationship with your brother like? Would it ruin the relationship because he would feel like he can no longer trust you, or are you afraid that he will be angry with you?

I believe your brother knows that what he is doing is wrong, but the temptation of all the inappropriate material on the Internet is very strong. I don't think the issue is knowledge. It is about the incredible pull of the *yetzer hara* and not being able to resist. Knowing and acting are two different things.

You can help your brother help himself, but you will not be able to stop him if he is intent on continuing his behavior. He will simply find another way to do it, a way that he will hide very well. It is important to try, though, and here are a couple of suggestions.

You can comment how difficult it is for *you* to steer clear of all the inappropriate stuff on the Internet. Use the discussion to express *your* concerns. Get him talking about the issue. Get him thinking about the seriousness of it, what it can do to a marriage, to a person's spirituality, etc. Since the conversation won't be directed at him (it is about you), he will not feel threatened.

You might also say that since it is so difficult for you, you will put up a sign near the computer that will remind you to "stay holy." Obviously, the sign will be helpful for anyone who is using the computer inappropriately.

If your brother is open to it, there are also technological interventions that would be helpful. Things like parental control programs, accountability programs, and similar software. Using these programs simply makes the challenge of dealing with the *yetzer hara* easier.

Also, is there someone who your brother looks up to and respects? Is there a tactful and discreet way for him to somehow get involved?

May G-d reward you for your efforts in helping your brother.

Rabbi Hochberg

Dear Rabbi,

My friends and I were discussing the following question. However, before I ask our question, I just want to assure the rabbi that this is only a theoretical discussion because we would never be able to live with ourselves if we did this! In fact, my friends don't even speak to boys. But we do have this question and we want to know what you think.

Our question was what if a girl would immerse in a mikveh before marriage? Does she still have to be shomer negiah? I thought I had this whole thing clear in my mind, but after talking to my friends, I am not so sure anymore. Can the rabbi help us out?

Leah

Dear Leah,

There are a couple of important points I want to respond to in your letter, so let's address the halachic issues first. Once a girl has her period, she remains in the status of *niddah* until she goes to the *mikveh*. Intimate relations with a woman who is a *niddah* is punishable by *kareis*, spiritual excommunication. (There are different opinions as to what exactly this means, but suffice it to say that it is a very, very bad thing.) If a girl goes to the *mikveh* (and follows all of the appropriate and extensive laws relating to going to the *mikveh*), then the punishment is no longer *kareis*. It becomes, according to some authorities, a rabbinic prohibition that is punishable by flogging, as the *beis din* sees fit. According to other authorities, there is also a Torah prohibition involved. The laws of *shemiras negiah* continue to apply even if a woman went to the *mikveh*.

However, let's leave the halachic issues aside and focus on another aspect of your question.

Marriage is special. (It is interesting to note that in almost all religions, it is the clergy, the spiritual and holy leaders, who create the marital bond between man and woman.) It allows two people to share the closest expressions of trust and intimacy within a holy framework. In fact, this is part of the reason why many people have a fear of commitment. Saying yes to one's spouse means that I am saying no to every other potential relationship out there.

Can you imagine how special and beautiful that commitment and relationship will be when you and your intended say yes to each other and only to each other?

Remember, there is only one special "first time" for everything. After that, it is no longer a unique experience. Even worse, it becomes the yardstick to which you compare other experiences.

Think of the specialness and uniqueness that lie ahead for you when you are patient.

Trust me, it's worth it.

Rabbi Hochberg

Dear Rabbi,

Please explain to me why women are treated so differently than men in the Jewish religion. I know that women are exempt from the time-related halachos and I understand the reason for that.

However, no one has ever explained to me why I cannot be alone with a member of the opposite gender. I am not looking for the moral reason. I am looking for the halachic reason.

Also, why are men and women not allowed to sit and daven together in a shul according to the Torah? Doesn't that seem old fashioned? Can't you be spiritual without acting like it's the Victorian Age? Could you please explain to me the reason for a mechitzah?

Yehuda

Dear Yehuda,

It is important to keep in mind that the key word is "different." Not second class, not underprivileged. The Torah treats women differently from men. Each has their own unique role to fill in G-d's grand master plan.

As far as your question goes, the halachic reason we cannot be alone with a member of the opposite gender depends on your relationship to that person. If it is someone whom the Torah forbids you to marry, then it is a Torah prohibition to be alone with her. It is derived from a *derash,* a means of interpreting the words of the Torah to understand some of its laws. If it is someone you are technically allowed to marry, it is a rabbinic decree dating back to the time of King David.

The reason men and women are not permitted to daven together is because prayer is a time to develop one's relationship with G-d. It requires concentration and focus. This is very difficult to do when you are seated next to a member of the opposite gender, or even if they are seated near you without a separation.

A *mechitzah* is not a segregation of women. It is a sanctification of your relationship with G-d. When you are in a shul, focus on that relationship.

Rabbi Hochberg

Dear Rabbi,

I have a problem and was wondering if you could help me.

What should you do if you get emotionally excited when you see her because she is really gorgeous? She doesn't have a clue how I feel, and I'm too afraid to tell her, because if she doesn't have the same feelings for me, I will get very depressed. Also, I'm only eighteen, and I am not going to be thinking about marriage for a few more years. What if she is already married to someone else by then?

I am a frum person, I am shomer negiah, and don't really have a strong need to touch her. But I love to see her and talk to her! I don't know what to do. I feel guilty, as a religious Jew, to think about her in this way. Everyone tells me it's natural, and I know it is. But I don't know how much more I can take. I don't mean physically; I am very much in control of my shemiras negiah and wouldn't touch her. I just want so desperately to be with her, talk to her, and be loved by her!

I spoke to another rabbi about this and he told me that our sages said that when a Jew is not engaged in Torah study, he immediately becomes vulnerable to attack by all the temptations of this world. Without Torah, a Jew can be overwhelmed in life's ongoing battle. Only through Torah does he have the means to overcome his evil inclination. So I should try to study more.

I agree completely with what this rabbi said, but what do I do about the feelings I have for her? They still aren't going away!

Please help me, rabbi. This is tearing me apart.

Shalom

Dear Shalom,

Thank you for sharing your difficult situation. I believe that, with G-d's help, there are several things you can do to make this easier. However, before I share my suggestions, I would like to make an observation.

Your letter gives me the impression that the main focus of your struggle is not sexual in nature. You made it very clear that you are *shomer negiah* and are determined to be strong on that issue. You said that your need to touch this girl isn't strong at all and your *shemiras negiah* is under control. You also expressed your intense need to see her, talk to her and be loved by her. These needs, to be loved and appreciated by this girl, are emotional needs. Knowing that a girl really cares about you is almost guaranteed to make you feel good inside, especially if you are a teenager.

Based on that, I suggest the following: In my opinion, since it is the guilt that is tearing you apart, this is what needs to be addressed first. On the one hand, you are experiencing very strong feelings for her, and on the other hand, you are feeling extremely guilty for having those feelings.

My approach in this situation would be to focus on dealing with the guilt. You see, G-d created people with powerful desires and they are just as much a part of the world as anything else. Our goal in this world is to control our actions when we have those desires. That is the key. You need to differentiate between *having* a feeling (which is normal and you should not feel guilty about) and *acting* improperly on the feeling (which is wrong and should be accompanied by guilt). It sounds like you are having some trouble differentiating between the two and this is causing you incredible stress and guilt.

Try to find some time and really explore this idea. Once you recognize that it is normal to have the feelings (*hirhurei aveirah*, thoughts of sin, from which no person is saved — see *Bava Basra* 164a) and you focus on what you do when you experience them, the guilt will quickly subside. You won't feel as tortured for having the feelings.

Of course, there is a difference between having the thoughts drift into your mind and intentionally replaying them again and again. It may also be helpful to read the chapter "Mind Control" where this concept is discussed in more detail.

Once the guilt is taken care of, you can move on to the next step of dealing with your relationship with this girl. Please let me know when you are ready for this step and we can work through it together.

Rabbi Hochberg

Dear Rabbi,

I just wanted to thank you for the great advice. So far, your advice has been the best and most thorough I've found, and I hope you will continue to give advice to people who need it.

Here's my question:

What if (yeah, right, like this is really hypothetical!) you believe that you found your bashert? The problem is you are only sixteen, but you know she is the one. You aren't only attracted to her looks, so it's not like that is the only reason for thinking that she is your bashert. She has many qualities that you like and find attractive.

Is this possible? Should I tell her how I feel? This whole question may sound ridiculous, but I want to know the answer from a Jewish perspective.

Donny

Dear Donny,

I have no doubt that you are attracted to this girl. And I have no doubt that there may be certain special aspects to this girl besides her looks that attract you. However, I find it hard to believe — and I think you will agree with me — that at age sixteen you know for certain that she is "the one," to the exclusion of anyone else.

Am I right?

The relationship and attraction that develops at age sixteen are very different from the ones that develops at age twenty-two, for example. Yes, you are attracted to her and you feel there is a relationship there. But no, it does not necessarily mean that she is "the one."

By the way, your comment that you are experiencing an attraction that is not based on looks was very mature. Not many people your age are able to see that. Very insightful.

What should you do? If I were you, I would sit tight and see what happens as you both mature.

You never know...

Rabbi Hochberg

Dear Rabbi,

I saw your essay about attraction and wanted to ask you something. Recently, I have been struggling with the idea of shemiras negiah and other such laws. On the one hand, I believe and understand that these mitzvos are important and need to be followed. On the other hand, it isn't so easy to keep them! Is it a sin to violate the laws established as "fences" around the Torah such as not being alone with a boy?

The reason I'm asking yet another rabbi (I have asked others about this question) is because, quite honestly, I need to find a solution that is acceptable in G-d's eyes and that I am happy accepting.

Rikki

Dear Rikki,

I would be happy to answer your question, but before I respond, I am curious about something you said. You mentioned that you are asking "yet another rabbi" because you need a solution that you are happy accepting and that is acceptable in G-d's eyes.

I am not sure what you meant by that. Can you tell me a little more? It may make it easier for me to answer your question.

Rabbi Hochberg

Dear Rabbi,

What I meant was that I have asked various rabbis and they have given me different opinions. I would be happy accepting something that would allow even small physical gestures such as holding hands. I would only be happy, however, if it falls into what the Torah permits.

Rikki

Dear Rikki,

It sounds like you are looking for an answer that will satisfy your physical desires and your spiritual desires at the same time.

Unfortunately, it doesn't quite work that way.

But let me ask you a question that may help put things in perspective.

It sounds like you have a good relationship with G-d, since you are looking for an answer that is acceptable in His eyes. If you knew that you could give G-d tremendous pleasure, so to speak, by doing what He wanted, would you do it? Would you forgo your own happiness in order to give G-d happiness?

Controlling our physical desires for no other reason other than that is what G-d wants, gives Him great pleasure, so to speak. In return, He provides us with unimaginable spiritual blessings and rewards.

I understand that physical desires can be quite powerful and sometimes feel almost impossible to control. But thinking of it this way may make it a little easier.

Of course, there are also many practical benefits to being *shomer negiah*. You get to develop a relationship with someone without the pressure of the physical part. You get to see what someone is really like as a person, not just how they make you feel at that moment.

There are some great books out there on the topic of *shemiras negiah* that discuss these issues in more detail.

Rabbi Hochberg

Dear Rabbi,

I read your essay "Attraction and Desire" and agree with it completely. My problem is that its effect will have worn off by tomorrow morning. It will be as though I never read it. Now that

I think about it, most things are that way with me. For example, I will attend a lecture about the importance of speaking properly. I listen to what the rabbi says. I promise myself that I will do it and I really mean those promises. However, the next morning, I wake up and the desire to be careful about my words is gone.

I really want it to work. I know it's the right thing. I don't think there's something wrong with me. Any advice would be deeply appreciated.

Sara

Dear Sara,

Inspiration is a tricky thing because it always wears off after a while. The key is to change your actions when you are feeling inspired, so that when you are no longer feeling that way, you will already be in the habit of doing good, positive things. This is the way to use inspiration successfully.

However, it can also be helpful to just go ahead and do something, even if there is no inspiration or feeling behind it. For example, with speaking properly, it may seem that you have no desire or feeling, but it is helpful to go through the motions anyway.

Of course, it would be wonderful if we always had enthusiasm for serving G-d in all that we do. However, sometimes it can be helpful to jump-start that process by going through the motions regardless of the feeling.

The feeling usually follows the thought which usually follows the action.

Rabbi Hochberg

Dear Rabbi,

Well, I really liked your essay because it was so thorough. I did have a question on the part where you discussed doing the right thing and that a good feeling would result from that. You mentioned it specifically for not secluding yourself with someone.

Meaning, if you refused to be in a yichud situation, you would feel good about the decision because you said no and did the right thing.

My question is if you would love to have yichud with someone and you never do it because G-d said not to, where is the good feeling? I think you will always have the feeling that you're missing out on something. Your imagination will paint this picture in your head that it could have been amazing, and you will never know.

Is it wrong to have both feelings at the same time? The feeling that you want to have yichud, but you won't, and the feeling that you are missing out if you don't?

Michal

Dear Michal,

There is always the feeling that it would have been a great experience if I did *xyz* (in this case, *yichud*) and now that I didn't, I am missing out. That is exactly how the *yetzer hara* entices us. However, the feeling of self-control that comes from doing the right thing can be used as a means of balancing the feeling that you missed out on something.

Human nature, being what it is, means that you will feel both emotions and that's perfectly normal. In fact, in order for you to have *bechirah*, you *have* to have both feelings pulling you in opposite directions. The Torah expects you to control what you do with that feeling, not necessarily to control having the feeling in the first place.

Rabbi Hochberg

Dear Rabbi,

I don't understand something you said. How many times are we faced with being alone with another person? How many different situations arise during the course of one simple day: an appointment with a doctor, a discussion with teacher, or having a service technician come to fix your telephone?

We do not go around thinking of everyone we see or meet in

a sexual way! Are you suggesting that we should look at these
situations as threats to our morality and spirituality?

Devora

Dear Devora,

The Rabbis were well aware that there are times when we are alone with others. There are specific laws that cover the details of when and where one is (or isn't) permitted to be alone with a member of the opposite sex. These are called the laws of *yichud,* and the situations you described are discussed within these laws.

I am not suggesting that you view every person you meet as a potential threat to your spirituality and moral values. But I do suggest that you need to be *fully* aware of the attraction between men and women and how that can impact your life. Specifically, the Torah provides guidelines to follow that make it easy to do just that.

However, even within the scope of the Torah's guidelines, be aware of any feelings, attraction, or emotions you experience when meeting another person. For example, if a man finds himself meeting a woman for a business lunch (in a permitted way) and all he can think about for the rest of the day is the next time he will see her, he needs to be aware of that.

My point is simply that you need to know yourself and your feelings and act accordingly. It will make your life easier.

Rabbi Hochberg

HABIT FORMING

I am a creature of habit.

As I pulled up to my house the other day, I noticed there was a car parked right in the spot where I usually park. It was no big deal — I parked about twenty feet away. But, as I walked up the stairs to my house, I realized that something was bothering me. Something didn't feel right.

I realized what it was before I reached the door. I didn't park where I usually park.

Logically, it made no sense for me to be feeling...well, annoyed would be the best word. I parked twenty feet away. It wasn't as though I had to park around the block or take a bus back to my house.

But I didn't park in my usual spot. There was an action that I had become accustomed to doing, a habit, and for a minute or two, it didn't feel right when I couldn't follow my routine.

Habits are a powerful force that can act as a double-edged sword. Habits can help motivate you to accomplish almost anything — but they can also prevent you from succeeding.

Let me explain. Most of your actions in a given day are based on habit. You get up at a certain time, and have a morning routine that you usually follow (and no one had better interrupt that routine if they know what is good for them). You have a favorite seat in the cafeteria, a certain writing style, a place where you always go to relax, and so on.

These are all habits. If you were to decide tomorrow to change one of your habits and do things differently, it would feel a little odd. Perhaps not very much. You might barely notice it. But for a few moments, something would feel a little out of place.

The power of a habit lies in its ability to lock you into a routine and make it extremely difficult to break out of that routine. Now, that's great when it is a good routine. For example, let's say you are careful to consistently daven at a certain time every morning, or that you visit an elderly person every Tuesday afternoon. Once you have developed that habit, it will continue to be strengthened each time you repeat it. The first few times may be difficult, but by the time you have done it twenty or thirty times, it will be much easier.

In fact, you can accomplish almost anything you want using the power of habit. Decide what you want to achieve and begin performing the steps to accomplish it. Make it into a habit. For example, suppose you decide that you want to speak respectfully to your parents. First, plan on talking to them respectfully for fifteen minutes, starting at 8:30 a.m., every single day. Be consistent. Soon it will become second nature. Now you can extend the time to a half hour, then an hour. The more consistent you are in your routine, the stronger the habit becomes, and the easier it is to continue the habit.

However, the power of habits can also be used in the opposite way. People can develop habits of doing the wrong thing and it becomes almost impossible to break out of the routine. For example, have you ever cheated on a test? Do you remember the first time? It was probably a difficult thing to do. You probably felt guilty and angry at yourself after the test. How about the second time? The third? You may have noticed that it became easier and easier. Soon it may (hopefully not) have become routine for you, part of the test-taking process itself.

You may have found this to be true with other forbidden actions. The first time you do something wrong, you are plagued with guilt and promise yourself it won't happen again. The second time is easier and the third time is easier still. The Talmud (*Sotah* 22b) says it very well: "The second time a person sins, it appears to him as though it is actually permitted." Pretty insightful. Does that concept apply to you?

Here's the secret to using habits. You see, there is another aspect to habits. Habits remove your thought process from the action. They make you do things without thinking, and once you are accustomed to doing things in a certain way, you will continue to do them that way even if it may not be logical or make any sense.

This is a practical method to jump-start your growth as a person. Don't stop to analyze whether or not you should do mitzvos, give charity, or pray. *Just do it.* Make the mitzvos and good deeds in your life into habits. Don't stop to think about them. Once you have developed positive habits, then you can begin to reflect on their deeper meaning. The same is true for breaking bad habits. Go through the steps to change the habit without thinking too much about it or asking yourself whether or not you should do it. Remember to always replace bad habits with positive ones.

The power of habits is their momentum, and the strength and ease they give to your actions. Use them to your advantage and become a creature of great habits.

READERS RESPOND

Dear Rabbi,

I read your essay on habits and I do agree with most of what you said. Yet, something at the end of it bothers me. You said that we should do the right things (i.e., mitzvos) and not think about or analyze them. I understand that we should do mitzvos first (without questioning G-d) and only later on begin to analyze them (similar to what the Jews did when they received the Torah. They said "Na'aseh v'nishma — we will do and we will understand"). However, there is a danger to doing that. We may become stuck in the habit of going through the motions of the mitzvah and not take the extra step of understanding what it is that we are doing. Take davening, for example. We should daven every day and at the appropriate times, yet, when one does not think about it, and is just doing it as part of his routine, it doesn't have as much significance to him.

I believe that if a person has the proper yiras Shamayim and bitachon, then I don't think analyzing a mitzvah would lead the person to not doing it, or prevent the person from growing. In fact, I think it would do quite the opposite. Analyzing the mitzvah will help a person acquire a greater appreciation for the mitzvah.

Chaim

Dear Chaim,

You are absolutely correct. Performing a mitzvah with the proper understanding and appreciation is the highest form of service to G-d. It is a level that one should always strive to reach. In the essay, however, I was referring to people who have trouble doing the mitzvah in the first place and need to jump-start their performance of that particular good deed. In that situation, the best thing to do is simply perform the mitzvah without analyzing it.

For example, someone who has trouble davening, should begin by simply going through the actions. Say the words even if you don't appreciate what you are saying. After you have become accustomed to performing the mitzvah, you can begin to analyze it.

However, in the situation you described, where you are doing the mitzvah and are looking for more, the proper approach is as you suggested, namely, to increase your understanding of the mitzvah. This will bring you even closer to G-d.

Rabbi Hochberg

Dear Rabbi,

I liked your article about habits but I had a question. What if someone has a bad habit of not davening, for example? She just might not want to daven. She has no interest in davening. She doesn't even want to do what you suggested, to "just do it." She is too stuck in the bad habit to try and change it. What would be a proper way of getting her interested in taking the steps to want to change the bad habit of not davening?

Rachel

Dear Rachel,

Make it meaningful. Make it apply to you. For example, you can focus on an area in your life that you would like some help from G-d. It could be health, relationships, money, friends, etc. Use extra concentration during the corresponding *berachah* in the *Shemoneh Esrei* that applies to your particular situation. This will give your davening significance and meaning in that particular area. Then, slowly, you can expand your focus, step by step, to include other parts of davening. Go slowly. It is the quality that is important at this point and will have the most impact on changing this habit.

Rabbi Hochberg

NAVIGATING LIFE SUCCESSFULLY

M any years ago, in Jerusalem, a young boy approached the great rabbi, Rav Yosef Chaim Sonnenfeld, with a question.

"Rabbi," he began, "I don't understand something. At the end of the Shabbos morning prayers we say '*Ein Keilokeinu* — there is no G-d like our G-d.' In the next verse we say '*Mi Ke'Elokienu* — Who is like our G-d?' Shouldn't the order be reversed? First, we should ask 'Who is like our G-d?' and then we can answer: 'There is no G-d like our G-d.' Wouldn't that make more sense?"

Reb Yosef Chaim smiled at the young boy. "Excellent question," he said. "However, before I answer you, I would like to ask you a question. Have you ever explored the ancient underground caves and tunnels beneath the Old City of Jerusalem?"

The boy nodded. "Of course, I have."

Reb Yosef Chaim continued, "You know that those caves can be quite dangerous. They are full of surprising twists and turns and people have gotten lost inside. Aren't you afraid of getting lost? How can you be sure that you will make it out safely?"

"Well," the boy replied, "before I go inside the caves, I attach a rope, a lifeline, to my waist and secure it to a large rock at the entrance. That way, I can explore the tunnels as deeply as I want and always make it back safely. I just follow my lifeline."

"You have just answered your own question," Rav Yosef Chaim told the boy. "The question of 'Who is like our G-d?' is a very difficult question. People who begin to explore that question can find themselves in great spiritual danger. Yet, one can and should ask that question. There is only one safe way: Tie a lifeline around yourself before you ask it. 'There is no G-d like our G-d' is your lifeline. It is your anchor. Secure that thought in your mind and you can safely explore the difficult question of 'Who is like our G-d?' You know that if you get confused, you can always return to your lifeline. You may get scared. You may wander into dangerous spiritual territory. Yet, you will be safe because you have a lifeline."

This story opens up some powerful ideas. Life can be very challenging and, as you move through it, you may encounter dangerous areas. Areas that can be dangerous to your spirituality, your emotions, your ability to make good decisions, even your physical health. There are many potential pitfalls. How are you going to make sure that you can navigate life safely?

The answer is simple but effective. Create and use lifelines. Use your family, your friends, your teachers, and your role models. Anchor yourself firmly and securely to them. Once you are anchored and have the necessary support, you can explore areas that may be too dangerous to explore on your own. You know that if you have questions or problems, you can always rely on your lifelines.

They can make all the difference.

READERS RESPOND

Dear Rabbi,

I kind of agree with what you are saying, but I don't feel like doing the whole lifeline thing right now. I want to continue having a good time and at some point later on...I don't know when...I'll look for some lifelines.

You only live once. I want to make it count, and at this point in my life, I want to party.

Michael

Dear Michael,

It sounds like you have decided to have a good time now. I won't try to change your mind.

I just want you to think about something. Picture the people who care about you as a boat in the middle of the vast ocean of life. You want to jump into the water and swim away from the boat for a short while? That's your decision. Just make sure that when you want to return to the boat, you are close enough to grab the lifeline they throw to you. You don't want to be so far away that it will be impossible for you to catch it, no matter how hard you try.

Good luck, Michael. As you said, you only live once...so please don't swim too far away.

Stay in touch.

Rabbi Hochberg

Dear Rabbi,

I love what you wrote about the whole idea of lifelines and I could definitely use some in my life.

I have a question. How do I know if the lifeline I choose is the right one? What if I attach or anchor myself to a particular person, but she is not a good lifeline? How can I make sure that my lifeline is the best one for me?

Esti

Dear Esti,

Like so many decisions in life, you have to give it your best shot, and have faith in G-d that you made the right decision. However, to make it a little easier, here are some guidelines for choosing a lifeline. The person you choose may have all or some of these qualities.

1. Make sure the person is someone you can relate to and understands you.

2. The person should be someone to whom you can comfortably ask your questions honestly and openly, without being afraid of his/her response.

3. The person should have the Jewish values, character traits, and strengths that are important to you.

4. The person you choose should be a role model for you, someone you can look up to and respect.

5. You have to be willing to learn from the person.

Also, keep in mind, that you can have many lifelines. For example, you may have a friend who is very careful about only speaking the truth. You can use her as your lifeline for that particular area of your life. You may have a teacher with whom you can openly discuss anything on your mind and who understands you very well. Use that teacher as a lifeline for another area of your life.

May G-d help you choose wisely and may you be able to serve as a lifeline for someone else one day.

Rabbi Hochberg

THE SOUND OF MUSIC

A hhh...the sound of music.

It is one of the few things out there that has the power to really get inside of us. Music can dramatically change our mood, evoke a long-forgotten memory, provide us with a place to escape, or just help us relax. We use music to exercise, to meditate, and to relax. The vast range of available musical sounds and melodies is incredible. From the sweet sounds of Shlomo Carlebach to the strong beat of hip-hop, from the instrumental melodies of Yanni to the tunes of Mordechai Ben David, music has a powerful effect on us. In fact, music was a central part of the service in the *Beis HaMikdash*. Imagine...hundreds of Levites with beautiful voices singing in harmony as all kinds of musical instruments are playing in the background.

It was the greatest concert in the world.

There is a story told about a student of the Baal Shem Tov (the founder of the chassidic movement who lived in the 1700s) who had a beautiful voice. He always led the prayers in the Baal Shem Tov's shul on Friday night.

One Thursday, this chassid was traveling back from another city, and he spent the night at an inn. The Polish peasants in the inn were quite drunk and were singing a very captivating tune. The *chassid* soon found himself singing along quietly with them, and the tune kept running through his head all night. As he saddled his horse and made his way back home the next morning, the tune continued to play in his mind .

That Friday night, the student assumed his usual place at the front of the shul and began to lead the congregation in prayer. As he was about to begin "*Lechah Dodi*," the only tune he could think of was the folk song that the drunken Polish peasants had been singing! He tried as hard as he could to think of another tune, but his mind remained blank. The crowd looked at him expectantly, waiting for him to begin. Finally, not knowing what else to do, he sang "*Lechah Dodi*" to the tune of the Polish peasants.

Afterward, he received a message that the Baal Shem Tov wished to speak with him privately in his study. The chassid entered and immediately began to apologize for his audacity in using a Polish folk tune for davening. The Baal Shem Tov raised his hand and smiled kindly at his student. "My son," he said softly, "let me ask you a question. We know that when the Holy Temple was destroyed, the Jewish people were sent into exile and scattered among the nations of the world. The holy vessels of the Beis HaMikdash, including the holy ark and the menorah, were also sent into exile and lost. Yet, what happened to all the beautiful songs that the Levites would sing daily in the Beis HaMikdash? Where have they gone? Why don't we remember any of them?"

The Baal Shem Tov continued, "The answer is that our precious and holy songs were also sent into exile and scattered among the nations. The melodies were turned into folk songs and exiled to taverns. I want to share something very special with you. The tune that you used this evening for "*Lechah Dodi*" was one of the holy tunes that the Levites used to sing. Unfortunately, it has been lost for twenty-five centuries. Tonight, you brought it back to our people. I thank you. Please, use this tune for the next several weeks so our people can learn it once again."

A fascinating story about one of the mysteries of music. Obviously, I am not suggesting that the contemporary songs of today are all long-lost tunes from 2500 years ago. But I do think that music is more mysterious and powerful than we might assume at first glance.

Why does music affect us so significantly? Some believe the reason is that it touches something spiritual, something intangible, within us. Others think that it impacts the right side of our brains, the artistic and creative side, in ways that logical thought cannot. Whatever the reason, music clearly affects the way we think, act, and feel, and can change our moods dramatically.

As a teenager, you probably listen to all kinds of music. Pay attention to music's influence on the way you act, think, and feel. The effects can be dramatic or very subtle (for example, the reason we don't do intense cardio workouts to classical music is because we need a hard tempo to help us move quickly). Music can make you more emotional or it can deaden your ability to feel someone else's pain. It can make you sleepy and relaxed or angry and upset. I challenge you to find a secluded area, listen to a sweet, slow, beautiful song, and not feel — even if it just lasts for a moment — an intense, emotional wave of feeling. I challenge you to listen to a heavy metal song while you are driving and not feel aggressive, pumped up, with a "need for speed."

The point I am making is simple: recognize that what you listen to affects you.

READERS RESPOND

Dear Rabbi,

I've heard this all before. It is standard yeshivah material and the truth is, I might even believe it somewhat. But this is why I have trouble with it: How do you know what inspires me? Many people, including me, don't really care for the regular Jewish music or classical music that's out there. For example, I took your challenge about listening to slow music and felt like throwing the radio out the window! It didn't move me at all.

I know quite a few people who feel the same way I do. Yes, I might listen to Shlomo Carlebach, but mostly I get my spiritual inspiration from rock music. I know that nowadays there is some crazy music out there with violent, racist, sexist, and anti-Semitic lyrics, but you could also put those lyrics to classical music. The music itself has nothing to do with the lyrics.

Jonathan

Dear Jonathan,

People are inspired by all kinds of things. To each his own. You are saying that slow, sweet music does not move you? That's fine. Every person has to find the key to what inspires him.

However, keep something in mind. Songs generally have lyrics and it isn't always so easy to keep the lyrics from popping into your mind uninvited. And how about the artist? There are all kinds of associations we make when we listen to music. Haven't you ever listened to a song and your mind instantly transports you back to a certain memory, a certain time, or a certain person?

How do you stop yourself from thinking about the artist or lyrics when listening to a song?

Doesn't that get in the way when you are trying to be spiritually inspired?

Rabbi Hochberg

Dear Rabbi,

One thing I don't understand. Music is not a mitzvah, so what is the difference where it comes from? If I can be inspired by a slow rock tune, why should I listen to Deveikus or Carlebach? Why should I have to set limits on what I do if it isn't a mitzvah?

Meir

Dear Meir,

True, music isn't a specific mitzvah. Neither is eating. Or sleeping. Yet, the Rabbis taught us in *Pirkei Avos* (1:3) that one should try to have all his actions *l'sheim Shamayim*, for the sake of Heaven (G-d). As Jews, we have the special ability to infuse even the most mundane actions with spirituality.

We should try to take advantage of this powerful ability.

Rabbi Hochberg

HOW TO STAND OUT
IN A CROWD

There you are, standing around with your friends, having a great time. You are all laughing, sharing a moment...you know the feeling. It is like you and your friends are the center of the world.

Friends are very important. They are so important that a great man named Rava once said, "There is an expression; let me have friends or let me die" (*Ta'anis* 23a). That's a strong statement. Yet, it shows us clearly that the Rabbis understood the power of friendship. We need friends. We need that interaction, that sense of belonging to a group. It is part of what makes us human.

Now let's take a closer look.

You are unique. Each one of your friends is unique. You have feelings and values that are important to you that may be very different from your friend's values. But something happens when you all get together. You can't really put your finger on it. It is just...well, it is just there. It is the feeling of being part of a group. It is the feeling of being connected to something greater and stronger.

Yet, it is something more than just being connected. It is the feeling of surrendering yourself — your thoughts, values, and feelings — to something much larger than you. You become a piece of something bigger.

It feels very good to be part of a group. People have tremendous influence over each other when they are together. Groups are a powerful force. However, what happens when the group wants to do something that goes against your values or that you believe is wrong?

It is very easy for me to sit here and tell you, "Just be strong and do the right thing. Stick to your values and principles. Develop positive self-esteem and you won't care what anyone says. Ignore the others." It may make sense in theory, but come on...that's not the way life works.

So here's some practical advice that does work...

Let's say you are standing in a group and they decide to do something that flies in the face of your values. Take a deep breath and turn to anyone in the group. Tell him exactly what you feel when you think about doing what was suggested. Don't tell him that it's the wrong thing to do. Don't tell him that it goes against your values. Tell him what is going on inside *your* head. How does going along with this idea make *you* feel?

You see, people can argue with you when you tell them they are doing the wrong thing. They can deny that their values are less than pure. But no one can argue with you about a thought or feeling that you have. It's your thought! If you tell them that it makes you sick to your stomach to think about doing *xyz* or you get so mad when someone says *xyz* that you want to punch a hole in a wall, they can't really argue with you.

What are they going to say? "No, you aren't feeling mad?" "No, you really *do* feel like doing *xyz*?" That's ridiculous! No one can argue with you over a feeling.

Here's an example. Suppose your friends decide that they want to sneak into a movie. You are uncomfortable doing that. So you say, "Look, guys, I feel very nervous about doing this. I'm concerned that we'll get caught, and even if we don't, I won't enjoy the movie, because I'll be constantly looking over my shoulder. I waited a long time to see this movie and I want to enjoy it. The whole idea makes me very, very uncomfortable." Then you sit back and don't say a word. Let your friends make the next move. They may try to convince you that there is no reason for you to be nervous, but if you just repeat again, "Thinking about doing this makes me very uncomfortable," what can they tell you? "No, it doesn't make you uncomfortable?" How can they argue with you over whether or not you feel uncomfortable?

This method puts you back in control. Simply describe how you feel and then sit back. You aren't judging them. You aren't backing out of the group. You are simply sharing your feelings and thoughts with them. And then you toss the ball right back at them. You can remain part of the group without giving in, because you are just presenting facts for the group to deal with.

Also, the chances are good that you aren't the only one in the group feeling uncomfortable. As soon as you start talking, someone else will probably jump in and say they feel the same way.

Obviously, this method does not work all the time. You have to use some discretion when you apply it.

But I think you will like the results...

READERS RESPOND

Dear Rabbi,

This question isn't really about peer pressure, but it is about friends, so I am going to ask it anyway.

I have a close friend with whom I have a lot in common. Sometimes (actually, many times), we get into trouble because we are so similar. Anyway, one day we got into a fight and we were really giving it to each other, and she said something that hit me like a bullet. I mean, it really stung! I got so upset, I walked away and now I can't make up with her. I don't even want to look at her or talk to her.

I know I shouldn't let it bother me so much and it is probably better that we aren't friends anymore, but it still hurts so much! I want to make up with her, but I feel guilty about doing it because we always get into trouble together. Maybe it is better if we don't make up. But then I feel so depressed!

Shevi

Dear Shevi,

I think I get the picture. Your close friend hit you with a very hurtful comment that stung terribly. You feel angry and depressed about not being her friend anymore, but you think that in the long run, this is the best situation for you. However, even though you know it will ultimately be good for you, it still hurts, and you feel guilty about letting it bother you so much since you know it will be good for you.

Well, let me suggest a few things:

First of all, realize that it is okay to feel hurt and angry when someone who you consider to be a close friend hurts you badly. We are human beings with feelings. Don't beat yourself up for feeling that way.

Second, if you said something wrong to your friend, you should apologize. You are not responsible for what she did, but you are responsible for what you did. Also, when you take the first step and apologize, usually the other person will respond warmly and apologize back to you. From that point on, the relationship usually instantly improves.

Now, I don't know you or your friend and I can't judge if your relationship is a good thing or not. That is for you to decide, either on your own or discuss it with someone.

Also, try to distract yourself and stay busy. Help someone out. Do the right thing. You will be amazed at how quickly you will start to feel better.

Rabbi Hochberg

GOOD GUILT AND
BAD GUILT

Q. How many Jewish mothers does it take to change a light bulb?
A. None, "I'll just sit here in the dark."

What is it about Jews and guilt? We've all experienced that heavy, depressing feeling of guilt. What is the Jewish perspective on guilt? Is guilt good or bad for you? Is it possible to feel too much guilt? How can you differentiate between the positive feeling of remorse and the incapacitating, negative guilt that shuts you down?

A friend of mine recently asked me for advice on this very issue. "You know," he began, "Rosh HaShanah and Yom Kippur are right around the corner. Although this is the time for *teshuvah* and for reflecting on the past year's deeds, I am faced with the same problem I had last year. As I review the past year, I find myself becoming more and more depressed. This depression feels so heavy that I lose all motivation to try to improve for the upcoming year. I feel like I have done such awful things and have so many *aveiros*, that G-d doesn't want to have anything to do with me anymore. Is this *teshuvah*? Is this the right way to feel? I know I should be feeling guilty about what I have done wrong, but this heavy, depressing guilt and sense of hopelessness is overwhelming. What should I do?"

We have all experienced the sometimes overwhelming feeling of guilt. Although guilt has many forms (for example: feeling guilty for doing the wrong thing, feeling guilty for not caring about someone else, etc.), I would like to focus on the delicate balance of *teshuvah* and guilt and discuss how it can be used as a catalyst for change.

The best way to begin is by understanding the function of guilt. Guilt is a powerful and healthy emotion that keeps us honest with ourselves. It is our safeguard for inappropriate behavior. It prevents us from continuing to do the wrong thing.

Guilt opens the door to *teshuvah*. You can't be expected to feel remorse for a sin you don't believe is wrong. You can't feel sorry for what you did if you don't feel badly about having done it. Guilt opens our eyes to the truth about our inappropriate and improper actions and makes us feel badly about them. It makes us think about our relationship with G-d and makes us aware that we may have hurt others by our actions. Guilt motivates us to change.

But not all the time...

We say every night in *maariv*, "... Remove the *satan* from before us and from behind us..." The meaning of removing the *satan* from before us is clear. We are asking G-d to prevent us from sinning. "Please, G-d," we pray, "protect us from falling into the hands of the *satan*." But what is the meaning of removing the *satan* from behind us? Once we have sinned, once the *satan* has accomplished his objective, what more does he want from us? Why are we asking G-d to remove the *satan* after he has already accomplished his goal?

The answer provides us with an insight into the way the *satan* operates. The *satan*'s approach in convincing us to do the wrong thing usually goes something like this: "It's not such a big deal. It's only slightly wrong. Just do it one time. One time won't really matter." Yet, as soon as we give in and do the wrong thing, he immediately switches gears and tries to show us the enormously damaging consequences of our actions. "Do you know what you just did? How can you ever hope to face G-d again? Do you think He wants anything more to do with you? Are you aware of the spiritual devastation caused by your actions? Don't waste your time trying to do the right thing anymore. You might as well give up."

Sound familiar?

You see, after we have done the wrong thing, the *satan* is just warming up. He desperately tries to make us feel depressed so that we will continue our improper behavior and dig ourselves deeper into the pit of despair and hopelessness. It is almost impossible to change when we have lost all sense of motivation. It is this strong, incapacitating guilt that we are asking G-d to remove when we say, "...Remove Satan from behind us..." This type of guilt is damaging and extremely unhelpful.

This is the challenging part: How do we determine the type of guilt that we are experiencing? Is it the healthy, positive emotion that helps us focus regretfully on our wrongdoings, helps us do *teshuvah*, and bring those lessons into the future? Or is it the negative, depressing guilt that keeps us obsessed with our past misdeeds and makes us feel worthless?

Here is a simple test, based on the above explanation. Ask yourself the following question: I did the wrong thing. I am sorry I did it, and I went through the *teshuvah* process...and now what? Is this feeling of guilt motivating me in a positive or negative way? Am I feeling so depressed that all I can focus on is my unworthiness and all that I have done wrong, or am I determined to move forward and succeed the next time? The answer will help you decide what kind of guilt you are feeling.

If the guilt is the damaging, incapacitating kind, *don't listen to it*. This is not healthy remorse and regret; this is debilitating guilt that prevents you from improving and growing spiritually. It is another powerful tool in the arsenal of the *yetzer hara*.

In fact, Rav Nachman of Breslov points out that this is symbolized in the curse that G-d gave the serpent in Gan Eden that his sustenance would be the dirt (see *Bereishis* 3:14). The serpent represents the *yetzer hara*. The sustenance of the *yetzer hara* is the feeling of lowliness and depression that a person feels when he thinks of himself "like dirt." It is a formidable weapon that the *yetzer hara* uses most effectively.

Recognize the difference between positive guilt and negative guilt. Respond warmly to the feelings of motivation and the future-oriented perspective that *teshuvah* and positive guilt produce. Shake off the heavy, incapacitating feelings of depression and hopelessness that negative guilt creates and understand that it is the *yetzer hara* at work.

You will see an immediate change in the way you feel, and begin to look forward to improving your relationship with G-d.

READERS RESPOND

Dear Rabbi,

Your insight helped me a lot...thank you. But what if I'm depressed for no reason? You know, I just feel sad about things and it isn't because of anything I did. At least, I don't think so.

Chaya

Dear Chaya,

People get depressed for all kinds of reasons. Sometimes there are medical reasons for depression. Sometimes there are other reasons. Some of the reasons may have nothing to do with anything you did. In fact, it is normal for people to feel down once in a while. The problems start when being depressed gets in the way of your living your life.

I suggest reading the essay "Hard Stuff" for more discussion on this issue.

Also, there are two things that can make a person feel happy and fulfilled when they are feeling down. These two things are very effective and I encourage you to use them.

They are 1) doing the right thing, spiritually, emotionally, and physically, and 2) helping others.

Based on this, here are some suggestions for when you get depressed: Help someone out. Try to take care of someone else's needs. Every day, try to do the right thing three times and write it down. Read this list every day and watch it grow...daily...weekly...monthly...

Rabbi Hochberg

Dear Rabbi:

What if you have done the unthinkable? The worst possible aveirah? How do you repent for your behavior and move on with your life? How do you achieve teshuvah?

I can't go through my day for two minutes without thinking about what I have done wrong. Please answer me and tell me what I should do!

Ora

Dear Ora,

It sounds like you are carrying a great deal of "stuff" around with you. Although it is impossible to make specific suggestions without knowing the particulars of your situation, I suggest the following.

Renew and strengthen your relationship with G-d. Acknowledge to Him and to yourself that what you did was wrong, and then turn toward the future. Guilt is helpful only in the way that it motivates us in a positive manner. If it drags us down, it is the work of the *yetzer hara*. Speak to a rabbi with whom you can comfortably share what happened and ask his guidance. Perhaps you can describe it as "a friend's problem."

May G-d guide you in the right direction. Remember, *nothing* stands in the way of *teshuvah*, no matter how horrific your action was.

This is so important, so critical, I will repeat it:

Nothing stands in the way of teshuvah, no matter how terrible or awful your sin was.

Rabbi Hochberg

10

PARENTS

We are all familiar with the commandment to honor our parents. It's right there, carved in stone, the fifth of the Ten Commandments. It is a fundamental and logical mitzvah, one that you probably find easy to fulfill.

Right.

This is the real world. Sure, you can go through the motions of honoring your parents, but sometimes it can be difficult to express the true honor and respect that deep down you know they really deserve. After all, it is true that your parents did a lot for you, but on the other hand, do your parents really love you? Do they really understand you? And if the answer is yes, then why do you argue so frequently? And what about rules? Does it seem that you are always talking about what you can and can't do? What about the things that you don't want to share with them for fear of their reaction? How are you supposed to honor and respect your parents when it can be so challenging to relate to them? What does G-d want from you?

Great questions.

You are absolutely correct. You and your parents probably are having a hard time relating to each other. Your parents gave birth to you, raised you, love you... but they don't completely understand you at this point in your life.

Let me explain why.

The teen years are a time of transition. A transition from a time when your parents made almost all of your decisions for you, to a time when you begin to take responsibility for your own behavior. A transition from child to adult.

A time when you are becoming your own, independent person.

And if you think that this transition is very overwhelming for you, I assure you that your parents aren't having it any easier.

Think about it for a minute. As desperately as you are struggling to be in control of the decisions in your life, your parents are struggling just as desperately with the idea that you are no longer a young child. You are growing into an independent adult, and you want the freedom and independence that an adult enjoys. Your parents, on the other hand, are used to looking at you and dealing with you as a child. The real truth of who you are is somewhere in between, and both you and your parents are struggling to find that balance. This struggle isn't an easy one.

Do you see why you find yourself arguing so frequently about your freedom, decisions, friends, and independence?

Your parents love you and care about you. And they are struggling with this transition just as you are. So love them. Realize that they are trying. Do your best to include them and be open with them. Most importantly, try to work through this time in your life *with* them.

Sure, you could argue 24/7 with your parents. It just gets a little tiring, that's all.

Who wants to waste energy on that?

READERS RESPOND

Dear Rabbi,

Your essay on parents really hit home for me. Especially with regard to the rules part. My problem is that my parents are way too worried about me. They expect me to call home every hour that I am out at night and my curfew is 10:30 p.m. I want to be able to have a later curfew and more freedom. How do I convince them that they can trust me?

Yaakov

Dear Yaakov,

Trust is a funny thing, a sort of catch-22. On one hand, trust has to be earned. People have to learn that they can trust you. On the other hand, how are you supposed to earn a person's trust if they don't give you the opportunity to earn their trust?

I suggest the following: First, work on being trustworthy and responsible. You want to be the person who others point to and say, "He's a responsible guy." Second, find a good time, approach your parents, and tell them you want to talk to them about something important. Sit down with them and begin by pointing out areas of your life where you are responsible and trustworthy. Explain to them respectfully, that you understand that they deserve the right not to be worried about you all the time. By the same token, you would like to have more independence.

Is there a solution that will work for both of you? Are there ways that you could show them how responsible you are? What are they looking for that will tell them that they can trust you?

And, once you have earned that trust and they let you stay out later, what are you going to do to make sure that you continue to earn their trust? Set up the plan in advance so both you and your parents will know what to expect as you earn more of their trust and gain greater independence.

Good luck, Yaakov. Remember, we teach others how to treat us.

Rabbi Hochberg

11
MIND CONTROL

Are your thoughts truly a reflection of who you are? What about the thoughts and feelings that you can't control? Do those powerful emotions and desires that seem to surface without any conscious effort on your part truly reflect the real you?

Are you held responsible for dark thoughts, disturbing beliefs, and feelings that you can't control?

Imagine you are seated at your desk at school, when you overhear a conversation. It seems, according to the latest school rumor, that your good friend, Sara, was selected to have the lead role in the school play. Although Sara is a close friend, you can't help feeling jealous about her success. Not only that, but deep down, part of you believes that *you* should be playing that part. You're the one who really deserves it. To be fair, Sara is a talented girl and a hard worker. You're annoyed with yourself for being envious of your close friend. Aren't you bigger than that? Yet the feeling keeps gnawing at you...

Or perhaps you are at a friend's house and you notice that he has a

DVD lying on his desk that you have been dying to get hold of. You know that your friend would let you borrow it. But then again, he might not. You could take it home for the night and slip it back into his room the next day. He wouldn't even notice. But the DVD doesn't belong to you, and you aren't a person who steals. Come on, you're only borrowing it for one night! Should you take it anyway? The thoughts start flying through your mind. What are you going to do?

You didn't ask to have those feelings and thoughts in the above examples. They surfaced without any conscious effort on your part. Did you do something wrong?

In the last paragraph of the Shema, we are commanded, "Do not stray after your hearts and after your eyes" (*Bamidbar* 15:39). Exercise control, we are told, and don't follow after the desires of your heart. Don't allow yourself to become jealous, angry, lustful, or greedy. Don't have any other undesirable emotions or thoughts that are part of the human condition. Control yourself.

On the other hand, the Talmud (*Bava Basra* 164b) makes a seemingly paradoxical statement: "No person is saved from thoughts of sin." No one, no matter how righteous he or she is, can escape provocative thoughts. It is part of what makes us human.

So, how can G-d command us in the Shema not to stray after our hearts? Experiencing those dark thoughts and feelings is part of our human existence that He Himself created!

The answer lies in understanding the difference between having a thought and responding to the thought.

G-d created people with powerful desires, feelings, and thoughts. It is normal to experience provocative and distracting thoughts and emotions. However, it is *our response* to the thoughts and feelings that we are challenged to control. That is the essence of the commandment of not straying after our hearts and eyes. While the choice to experience the desire or thought may not be within our control, it is our responsibility not to act on it. We are expected to exercise self-control in our response.

Welcome to the world of free choice — of actions, not thoughts.

G-d doesn't expect you not to have any jealous thoughts whatsoever toward your friend and her success. He doesn't expect you to find it impossible to think about taking home the DVD. However, once you are consciously aware of what you are doing, once you are back in control, He pays close attention to what you will do next. Will your attitude toward Sara turn noticeably icy? Will you take the DVD? Or will you allow the thoughts and feelings to pass through your mind, perhaps even acknowledging them as they move along, and continue through your day? How will you respond when you experience envy? What will you do when you have a desire to take something that doesn't belong to you?

Our challenge lies in our response, not in the experience. The initial thought or feeling may not necessarily be in our control, but our response and subsequent actions are certainly our responsibility.

In fact, the aforementioned verse from the Shema, "Don't stray after your hearts and after your eyes," subtly points this concept out. When those dark and provocative thoughts enter your mind uninvited, don't concentrate and obsess over them. Allow them to leave. Don't stray *after* them, as they are passing through your mind. Let them go. It is only when we stray after them and respond the wrong way that we are taken to task.

How do we allow negative thoughts to leave our mind?

One of the great Jewish leaders of the previous generation Rabbi Yaakov Yisrael Kanievsky (the Steipler Gaon), *zt"l*, provided an answer in a letter to one of his students.

He wrote, "There is only one solution to this issue: distract yourself. The more you focus on preventing those thoughts, the more frequently they will invade your mind... it is a well-known fact that a person can only concentrate on one thought at a time. Therefore, distract yourself with another thought and the dark, provocative thought will disappear..."

A simple solution. And a highly effective one. Don't focus on the thought or feeling. Distract yourself. Allow the thought to leave your mind and move on.

Let's go back to the school play example and apply this idea. The conversation in your mind may go like this:

"I can't believe Sara is getting that part... I am glad for her... No, I am not! I should be the one playing that part!... Come on, Sara is a good friend. Be happy for her... It hurts, though. I am jealous of her success. Do you think she would be happy for me if I were the one who got the part? I don't think so...well, she might be happy for you... I have to stop thinking about this... Let's see...there's Leah. Let me go ask her about the history test next period."

Of course, this is not to say that one shouldn't strive to achieve great goals in managing one's emotions and thoughts. Raising the bar is always commendable. Keep in mind, however, that experiencing these thoughts and feelings is normal and part of the human condition that G-d created in His infinite wisdom.

READERS RESPOND

Dear Rabbi,

I just wanted to share a trick I once read in a book on meditation. Whenever you find yourself fantasizing or getting distracted by a thought, you just say to yourself, "Oh, well," and move on.

I have tried it and it really works. It is also a lot better than beating yourself up for having the thought!

David

Dear David,

Thanks for sharing that trick. I am glad you found it helpful. I always say, "If it works, keep doing more of it."

Spread it around.

Rabbi Hochberg

Dear Rabbi,

I just wanted to tell you that I felt a great sense of relief when I read your article. I was always angry at myself for thinking about things I shouldn't have and for focusing on those thoughts. Your article opened my eyes to the fact that I could have thoughts that weren't my fault. What a relief!

Thank you and thank you again!

Levi

Dear Levi,

I am glad you found the article helpful.

I would just like to clarify something that you mentioned. You said that you were angry at yourself for dreaming and for focusing on certain thoughts.

Having the thought or fantasy drift into your mind is one thing. Continually focusing on it and replaying it again and again is another.

If we keep replaying an improper fantasy in our heads intentionally, we can't exactly blame it on our human nature.

The best thing to do as you find the thought drifting into your mind, is let it go. Try some of the tricks mentioned in the article or distract yourself in some way. If you focus on not having the thought, you will only succeed in making it stronger. (You know what they say: The best way to think about flying pink elephants dancing around the room is to tell yourself *not* to think of flying pink elephants dancing around the room.)

Good luck, Levi.

Rabbi Hochberg

DOMINO EFFECT

id you ever set up dominoes in a row and gently tip over the first one? Depending on the arrangement of dominoes, you can get a pretty cool effect. I remember flipping through an old copy of the *Guinness Book of World Records* and seeing a picture of an entire gym filled with dominoes that were about to be knocked down. There were pictures, spirals, bridges, and races between two different colored lines of dominoes. It was amazing to me that knocking that first domino could set off a chain reaction of falling dominoes that would go on for almost an hour.

This is basic physics stuff; you generate a force and that force has an effect on something else, which affects something else, etc. Cause and effect. It is a law of nature and a law of life in general.

One of the hardest — yet very important — concepts to understand in life is cause and effect. We all have trouble with it. One of the great things about being a teenager, though, is that you can live for the moment and usually get away with it.

But let's explore this idea further. How many times have we done something that seemed like such a great idea at the time...and it may have been a great idea at the time...but we paid for it later? Even little things like staying up all night. We pay for it the next day when we can't keep our eyes open.

Or the time you did a small favor for a friend and two months later, someone offers you a job because of your action. Cause and effect. There is no action or decision we make that doesn't have some kind of consequence. The consequence can be good or bad, but there is no getting around the consequence.

So...what practical advice can I give you that will allow you to take advantage of this concept and help you make good decisions?

Try this. Let's call it the "Rule of Two" and this is how it works: Any time you are faced with a decision...and it doesn't matter if it is a major one or an insignificant one...ask yourself the following question: Even though right now I desperately want to do *xyz*, how am I going to feel about having done it in two weeks? Two months?

Think about it.

If your answer is "I will be glad in two weeks or two months that I did *xyz*," (or even "It won't make a difference in two weeks,") then chances are pretty good that doing *xyz* now is the right decision. However, if your answer is that after two weeks you are going to look back and realize that *xyz* was not a smart thing to do, then it is best to think long and hard before doing *xyz*.

I understand that the last thing you want to think about while having a good time is the consequences of your actions.

I challenge you to try.

READERS RESPOND

Dear Rabbi,

I liked your "Rule of Two" idea. But how I do force myself to think about the consequences when I am in the middle of something? If I thought about them, I probably wouldn't get myself into trouble. The problem is that I don't think about the consequences! How do I get myself to think about them when I am in the middle of doing stuff I shouldn't do?

Chani

Dear Chani,

You brought up a good point.

It is really difficult to stop yourself once you are in the middle of doing something you shouldn't be doing. That's almost in the superhuman category.

The trick is to think about the consequences *before* you get too involved in whatever it is that you are doing. Plan your moves before you jump into things and it is much easier.

Of course, you can (and should) always try to stop yourself when you are in the middle of something you know you shouldn't be doing. It is just easier to do it beforehand.

Rabbi Hochberg

13

A NEW LOOK AT SMOKING

L et me begin by explaining what I am *not* going to be discussing here. I will not talk about the health risks of smoking. There is enough information out there already on this topic and, besides, we all know teenagers live forever so it doesn't apply to you, anyway. Besides, if you are smoking or thinking about smoking, you already know the health risks and have decided to go ahead and smoke anyway. I am not going to change your mind by presenting you with medical evidence about the dangers of smoking.

Instead, I have a different challenge for you.

I want you to think about why you started smoking.

I bet that you did not enjoy your first cigarette. You may disagree, but I am pretty certain that if you are really honest about it, you will agree with me. You probably didn't even enjoy the second one. The third one? Maybe. So why did you smoke the first one? Why did you do something that you really didn't enjoy?

I am also willing to bet that you didn't smoke that first cigarette alone.

You were probably standing around with some friends, some who never smoked before and some who did smoke. A few of you lit up, you tried it, pretended you liked it (or maybe you didn't even pretend that you liked it). But you did it anyway.

So what made you light up for the first time? It's not because you enjoyed it...we already agreed on that. You smoked because you were subjected to the most powerful force in a teen's life.

Peer pressure.

A force that makes you act in a certain way, regardless of your real feelings and thoughts.

And you know, there might have been one person in the group who didn't try smoking. Sure, everyone tried to get him or her to do it. There was a lot of good-natured teasing, maybe even some malicious teasing, but he or she didn't give in. The teasing eventually died down, a few more comments were made, and then the conversation turned to something else.

How did you look at that friend the next time you got together? It was probably with a mixture of respect and jealousy. He or she didn't give in to peer pressure. He or she did something that you wish now you could have done.

Here's my point. I challenge you to be that person.

I also want to point out another reason why you might have started smoking. What better way to show your parents that *you* are in charge of your life and not them? You can do what you want. They don't want you to smoke because it is dangerous? You'll show them. It's your life...your health...and you will do what you want.

Sound familiar?

And you know what? It is your life. You are a teenager and you are trying as hard as you can to become your own person. Independent. Strong. In control of your own life.

I just want to make one small suggestion.

Pick something else. That's all. Find something that allows you to express yourself and your independence, and shows the world that you are your own person. Something that you can do to prove to yourself, your parents, and your friends that you are unique.

I don't think you should deny your uniqueness.

I'm just suggesting that you might want to think of a different way of expressing it.

And for those of you who have been smoking for a while, here's a question for you:

Why do you think it is so hard to stop?

I'm not referring to the physical addiction, although that is certainly a big part of the reason. I'm talking about the stuff that has nothing to do with the actual smoking.

Let me give you an example.

You are standing around with your friends after a ball game and everyone pulls out a pack. Yesterday you may have decided to quit smoking, but that is going to be really hard to do now. Why? Well, for one thing, it is hard to stand around, doing nothing, when everyone else is smoking. You feel stupid and who wants to feel stupid? It is much easier to do what everyone else is doing. No one wants to be different.

Here's another possibility: It may simply have become a strong habit, a habit that you can no longer fight. Or maybe you just enjoy the time to yourself. You enjoy being able to step away from everything going on in your world, and for a couple of minutes, it is just you and your cigarette. Perhaps you may be afraid of what you will do if you don't smoke.

There could be a lot of reasons why it is hard for you to stop smoking and the purpose of this chapter is not to give you a list of anti-smoking resources. When you decide that you are ready to stop smoking, you will find the resources you need.

I just want to get you thinking about a behavior that people usually do without thinking.

READERS RESPOND

Dear Rabbi,

Baruch Hashem, I am not a smoker, although I have friends that smoke both cigs and drugs. I've been with that crowd and have seen plenty of people take their first smoke. Been there, done that.

You hit the nail on the head. It is peer pressure. The fear of not being accepted and not having enough self-confidence to stand up for what you really believe. That's why I enjoy your essays so much. They are brutally honest, and although they are sometimes hard to accept, they hit you right between the eyes. Even if I disagree with you, they have an impact on my thinking.

Zev

Dear Zev,

I am glad you find the essays to be helpful, albeit brutally honest. It is said that part of the fire of Gehinom is the searing light of the truth.

Truth can burn sometimes. We tend to avoid that which causes pain, but at the end of the day, it is worth the discomfort.

Feel free to pass the essay along to anyone who you think would benefit from it.

Rabbi Hochberg

Dear Rabbi,

I love your stuff, but I have to take a stance on this one. From what I have noticed, contrary to popular belief, most people do not start smoking because of peer pressure or advertisements. I think most people start to smoke because it helps them relax. People also start smoking because they are curious what it is like, not because of peer pressure.

Stacy

Dear Stacy,

You are right about people smoking for relaxation. Nicotine acts as both a stimulant and a relaxant, and once a person starts smoking regularly he does it because his body needs it.

However, that is true once you have already started smoking. You and I both know that there is nothing relaxing about that first cigarette. You are stressed about trying it out and probably worried about getting caught. And even if you were simply curious and wanted to find out what smoking was like, you probably didn't smoke the first two cigarettes by yourself. I bet there were others around.

Please do me a favor, Stacy. Ask around and see how many people smoked their first two cigarettes alone. I would be surprised if it was many people. But let me know.

Rabbi Hochberg

Dear Rabbi,

I am an eighteen-year-old religious girl, and I have been smoking on and off since I was fifteen. A lot of what you said made sense and I have found to be true. However, not everyone starts to smoke because of peer pressure. I know that I started as my own form of rebellion. My experience with others is that smoking today is done more to relieve pressure than anything else. I certainly didn't start because it was "cool" to do it. I had my first cigarette at a family simchah when nobody else was around. Now I smoke because it relaxes me, and I do it privately.

Anyway, thanks for the essay and I hope some kids who would have started smoking will not start now. Also, can you suggest some alternative ways of dealing with the pressures of life besides smoking?

Hindy

Dear Hindy,

The stress and pressures of life can be overwhelming. Sometimes it can be one particular problem that is causing the trouble, yet it spills over into everything else that is going on, so your entire day seems overwhelming. Pay attention if this happens and try to deal with the real problem.

Personally, I have found exercise to be a great stress reliever. Some people turn to hypnosis or meditation. Read books on *bitachon* and *emunah*. Check out some "self-talk" books in the library. Find someone you can talk to, including friends, parents, teachers, and rabbis. And most importantly...*DAVEN*. You'd be amazed at what you can accomplish with *tefillah*.

I don't want you to think I am giving you "standard" answers; I firmly believe those suggestions will help.

However, if those suggestions don't work, we need to find some that do, so please keep in touch.

Rabbi Hochberg

MISCELLANEOUS THOUGHTS

Dear Rabbi,

Is there a good way to handle anger? I seem to lose it every time my sister-in-law gets me mad. I try to talk with her and be friendly to her, but we just don't seem to get along at all. Should I tell her to just stay away from me? Is there another way for me to handle the situation?

Esther

Dear Esther,

I am a firm believer that when we feel anger, or some other strong feeling, it cannot be hidden well. It may come out through our words or our actions, but trust me, it *will* come out in some way. You may find yourself driving faster than usual or snapping at your friends more easily, for example.

One of our life goals may be to improve our character to the point where we don't get angry. But that is a life goal. What should we do until that time? What should we do right now when the feeling is threatening to burst out of us?

One effective way of dealing with this is to get the feeling out there and put it right on the table. This way you get it out of you and you put it where the other person can respond to it.

In your situation, I suggest you describe to your sister-in-law how you feel when you get mad and what makes you mad. For example, if I were mad at you, instead of yelling at you and walking away, I would say (as calmly as possible), "When you do *xyz*, it makes me furious. I feel like getting up and walking away. It is so hard for me to sit still when you do that, because I want to yell at you."

Describe in detail what the person did and how it makes you feel. *just do it calmly.* It is not as difficult as it sounds and you will feel much better.

Rabbi Hochberg

Dear Rabbi,

I have a question that is really bugging me and I'm wondering if you can help me out. Recently, I read a story about a rabbi who used to smoke all the time. One Shabbos, he was offered a cigarette by a Russian officer. The rabbi told the officer that he had stopped smoking, and from that day on, in order to keep his word, he never touched a cigarette again.

Well, someone asked me last week if I watch TV, and I told her that I don't. The truth is I only said it because I hadn't watched for a long time and didn't intend to watch so much in the future. I certainly did not intend to make a promise not to watch again, because I know I will continue.

However, I really do want to stop, but I know it is not a realistic goal. Any suggestions?

Ahuva

Dear Ahuva,
The lesson from the story illustrates how careful we have to be with

our mouths and what we say. It is a wonderful goal to strive for and is truly the mark of a great man or woman who acts as the rabbi did in the story. Thank you for sharing that story with me.

You mentioned that you would like to watch less TV. The best advice is to jump right in and simply take it one day at time. It is a lot easier than telling yourself that you will never watch again. Reward yourself for the small accomplishments and build on your past successes.

May G-d help you achieve all of your goals!

Rabbi Hochberg

Dear Rabbi,

If Judaism is the truth, then why are we such a minority in the world? Wouldn't you think that everyone would want to seek out the truth?

Sharon

Dear Sharon,

That is a great question. In true Jewish fashion, let me respond with a question...

Tell me, assuming Judaism is the truth, would you seek it out? What would drive you to embrace it?

Think about the answers. They will help you develop a greater appreciation for G-d and Judaism.

There are also many wonderful books out there if you would like to learn more. I suggest reading *Beyond a Reasonable Doubt* by Rabbi Shmuel Waldman (Feldheim) and *Permission to Believe* and *Permission to Receive* by Lawrence Keleman (Targum Press).

Rabbi Hochberg

Dear Rabbi,

I was wondering if you could give me your opinion as to whether or not girls and women should learn Talmud. I'm sort of collecting opinions and seeing what the differences are and what the sources are, so I can make a decision.

Part of my problem is that the reason I thought women shouldn't learn Talmud, I don't believe anymore. That's why I want to either find a better reason why I shouldn't, or find out if it is something I should be doing. I mean, my school's philosophy is that going to college is better than learning Talmud! How can this be? Going to college is better than learning Torah?

Thank you for your time.

Batsheva

Dear Batsheva,

This is a complex halachic issue and each person must consult her rabbinic authority to find out what she should do. Some of the issues include whether or not there is a difference between teaching Talmud to a class of girls as part of a curriculum and a girl learning Talmud on her own because of a strong desire to increase her knowledge of Torah and G-d.

There have been women in history who have developed into extremely knowledgeable scholars. In fact, there is a story recorded several hundred years ago, where a woman by the name of "Rabbanit" Miriam used to say a *shiur* in the *beis midrash* for the students. They set up a small tent for her in the front of the room (for the sake of modesty) and she would say an advanced *shiur* (*Sha'alos U'Teshuvos Maharshal* 29).

However, to answer your question, there is something you need to explore honestly before you enter into the halachic discussion.

Are you interested *l'sheim Shamayim*, in developing a closer relationship with G-d, His will, and His Torah? Or are you attracted to the intellectual pursuit, or interested for some other reason? Do you want to learn Talmud because of a belief in the equality of the sexes, or do you simply have a burning desire to learn more?

Think long and hard about the answers and then discuss your particular situation with your rabbi.

Rabbi Hochberg

Dear Rabbi,

It seems that the Rabbis of olden times made numerous laws that are much stricter than the laws of the Torah, for example, yichud, not eating milk after meat, and many of the laws of Shabbos.

Do you think that they were right to make such laws? I know we are supposed to believe that they were much, much wiser than we are, but how can that be possible? Look at the technology of today versus the technology of a hundred or three hundred years ago! How could they have been smarter than we are today?

I really want to trust and believe in the rabbanim, and the fact is that deep down I do. I just have trouble with the idea. Can you help me understand this whole thing?

Yael

Dear Yael,

You are showing true strength by believing in something that is difficult for you to understand.

Here's one approach that may make this issue a little clearer.

Spirituality is not like technology. Technology's greatest strides occur as we move further ahead in time. As you pointed out, the technological advancements of today are vastly greater than the achievements of several hundred years ago. Our knowledge is built on the foundation of the knowledge of previous generations.

Spirituality, on the other hand, works in the opposite manner. The Torah was given to Moshe in all its glory, creating the zenith of spirituality. With the passage of time, we have been moving down from that spiritual peak ever since. Our Torah knowledge and relationship to spirituality today is incredibly more inferior to what people knew and experienced a thousand years ago.

So to answer your question, you are correct that we may have a greater knowledge of technology today than they did in the past. However, they had a much greater understanding of G-d, His Torah, and spirituality than we do.

Therefore, it is extremely important to trust in the *rabbanim* of the past and today. Not that they are infallible or immune from making mistakes, but they are better equipped to guide us in accordance with the Torah and G-d's will.

They are closer to the source.

You know, there is an interesting custom that is found among many of the martial arts. All of the students must refer to the instructor as "*Sensei*" (Teacher), "Mister," or "Sir," even if the student is ten or twenty years older than the instructor.

The reason is simple. You must have respect for a teacher if you are going to learn from him or her. Calling the instructor "Mister," showing respect for him and his knowledge, will help *you* absorb the lessons better.

It benefits you.

It may be helpful to adopt a similar approach when dealing with the laws the *rabbanim* have set up. We may not fully understand their reasons, but we must respect them and do our best to try to understand. The *rabbanim* had tremendous insight into human nature and that wisdom is reflected in their laws. If we don't succeed in understanding those laws, we must keep in mind that they were much greater spiritually than we are today, and they understood spiritual concepts that we might not perceive clearly.

I think this approach will make it easier to deal with this issue.

Rabbi Hochberg

Dear Rabbi,

I am sixteen years old and recently got into a huge fight with my parents over something. I found out that my mother read my diary without permission, and I blew up at her and told her that she had no business reading my stuff. She said that, as my parent, she has the right to go through my things to make sure I am not involved in anything dangerous.

What do you think, rabbi? Who is right?

Dena

Dear Dena,

It must have been very frustrating to find out that your private thoughts aren't as private as you thought. You feel that your privacy was violated when your mother read your diary. Your mother believes that she has every right to go through your things because she is your parent.

Who is right?

I have heard arguments from both sides of the fence. Some people believe that parents have every right to know what is going on in their children's lives because the children are their responsibility. Other people think that children have a right to privacy, and parents should not be allowed to go through their stuff.

Without getting into the discussion of who is right, here's a way to deal with this situation that will work no matter what side you think is correct.

Tell your parents that there is something very important that you need to discuss with them and you want to set up a time to talk. Once all of you are sitting down to talk, tell them you understand that, as your parents, they need to know you are safe. On the other hand, you really want and deserve your privacy. What can be done so they can feel comfortable that you are safe and you can feel comfortable that you have privacy that doesn't involve going through your things? Be creative and honest.

Use this discussion as a springboard for another discussion. Why does your mother think you might be involved in something inappropriate or dangerous? Does she trust you? If not, why not? What can you do to earn that trust? What needs to happen for her to give you the independence and trust that is so important to you?

Try to be as clear as possible about what each side will agree to do for the solution to work. Can your parents expect you to be open and honest about where you are going at night? Can you expect them not to read your diary anymore?

Keep it respectful and try to really understand the other person's point of view. (This is very important, or the meeting will quickly degenerate into a shouting match, and that won't be helpful to anyone.)

There will be times when you will slip up and they will slip up. Expect it to happen, and quickly try to move past those occasions and honor the agreement.

This approach will work if you keep it gentle and respectful and everyone involved wants to work this out reasonably.

Rabbi Hochberg

Dear Rabbi,

I have a lot of friends who constantly ask me to do things for them. I don't really mind because I am able to help, but it can get really annoying sometimes. I don't like to say no, but sometimes I wish they would just leave me alone! I am not looking for advice on how to say no...I can do that if I have to. I just want chizuk for the times I say yes, but I don't really want to! Help!

Shuli

Dear Shuli,

I once heard a story that gave me tremendous *chizuk* in this area.

There was once a wealthy man who was very generous, and he quickly found himself being constantly interrupted throughout the day by poor people who needed his help. After a while, he decided that it was too much and wanted to limit his involvement and help. However, he decided to ask the Chafetz Chaim before he made this important decision. He traveled to Radin, and as he entered the Chafetz Chaim's house, he saw that the Chafetz Chaim was giving a *shiur*. He sat down in a corner and listened.

The Chafetz Chaim was saying, "We say in *Tehillim* (23:6) 'May only goodness and kindness pursue me all the days of my life.' Why would a person run from goodness and kindness? Shouldn't he be pursuing those wonderful things instead of running from them?"

The Chafetz Chaim continued, "The answer is that every person has their struggles and *tzaros*, problems, in this world. Some people struggle with health. Some people struggle with relationships. Some people struggle with money. Some people struggle with children. We daven that our *tzaros* should come from a place of goodness and kindness. The poor man has the *tzaros* of never having enough money for food, and the rich man has the tzoros of being constantly interrupted by those less fortunate than him. Isn't it better to be the person who is in the position of giving and helping instead of the person needing to beg and plead from others? They are both *tzaros*, but we ask G-d that it should be the *tzaros* of having goodness and kindness pursue us, not the struggles of sickness and poverty. If a person didn't have the struggles that goodness and *chesed* provide, who knows what his struggles might be?"

The wealthy man stood up and left the room. He had his answer.

I hope this story provides you with the *chizuk* to continue the wonderful *chesed* that you do.

Rabbi Hochberg

Dear Rabbi,

I have an unusual question for you. I think I have discovered my true purpose in life!

I am only fourteen years old. My question is, if at such a young age, I accomplish my purpose, what will happen to me? Will G-d continue to keep me alive if my task in this world is completed?

Rivky

Dear Rivky,

I am glad that you have found a very special goal or purpose in your life that you believe is unique to you.

However, unfortunately, we do not have prophets today who can verify that what you think is your purpose is really your true purpose. So while you may think that you have found your purpose, the reality may be very different.

Also, how do you know that what you are thinking about is your only purpose? There may be hundreds more in the course of your life that you have to fulfill.

As far as what happens to you when you have accomplished your purpose, it's not that simple.

Here's my suggestion. Try to focus on doing the right things in life and follow what you believe to be your purpose.

Leave the rest up to G-d.

Trust me, He is looking out for you.

Rabbi Hochberg

15

HARD STUFF

O f course, there are also some unpleasant things we should probably discuss.

I am talking about the hard stuff, like feeling extremely depressed, or constantly obsessing over things, or being too afraid to talk in class because you are worried about having a panic attack, or thinking you are crazy.

I'm also talking about the scary and overwhelming stuff that no one likes to talk about. Stuff like drinking or using drugs, fighting with an eating disorder, or hurting yourself. Or perhaps you may have been hurt or abused by somebody and never told anyone. Maybe you have a friend or you know someone who is struggling with these issues. You desperately want to help and be helped, but you don't know what to do.

Dealing with these issues can be tough and terrifying.

You might find yourself feeling very alone, thinking that no one else is struggling the way you are struggling. You might be frightened by what you are thinking, yet at the same time enjoy having the thoughts. You may desperately want to feel better, but you can't even imagine what that would feel like — and you certainly don't think you are ever going to get there. You could be feeling all of these things or none of them.

But here's the problem.

There is no way I can cover all these things in a couple of pages. Not even close. Each one of these topics could, and probably should, have its own section, and that is way beyond the scope of this book.

So here is what I am going to do...

I want to talk about three main points that will hopefully give you a clearer perspective on getting help for these issues. They are general points, but think about them and apply them to your specific situation.

Point number one: You don't have to suffer.

There is no mitzvah that says you need to resign yourself to feeling depressed or to having an eating disorder. On the contrary, we are commanded to do our best to care for our physical, emotional, and mental health. Although there is reward for suffering, G-d expects us to take the steps necessary to get better.

You deal with enough difficult things in your life. Don't make life even harder by thinking you have to suffer with something like this.

Point number two: You do not have to struggle with an issue by yourself.

Come on, you won't face a history final without spending all week studying away with your friends. How in the world do you expect to manage something that affects you so deeply all by yourself? This is not the kind of struggle you want to handle on your own.

In fact, the Talmud (*Yoma* 75a) encourages people to speak things over with others when they have a problem.

Family and friends can often be tremendous sources of strength, support, and encouragement. If necessary, find professional help for the problem you are facing.

But don't face it alone.

Point number three: You are not the only person dealing with this.

It happens all the time. Just last week I was working with a girl who was very upset about having to get professional help for her situation. "It's crazy!" she burst out. "Why am I the only girl my age who has a stupid problem? What's wrong with me?"

That's when I told her that last week nearly ten girls her age sat in the exact same chair she was sitting in now. And at least five of those girls shared a similar, if not worse, problem than the one she was facing.

There is comfort in numbers. There is comfort in knowing that you are not the only one facing a tough and upsetting issue. The odds are really good that a lot of other people have dealt with and are dealing with the same stuff and, more importantly, have successfully moved past it.

READERS RESPOND

Dear Rabbi,

My parents told me I need to go for counseling. What's up with that? I don't have any mental problems! Why do I have to go for help?

Michal

Dear Michal,

I'll let you in on a little secret.

There are a *lot* of people who go for help, and they don't have any mental problems at all.

So why do they go?

They go because sometimes the bumps in the road of life get too intense.

Did you ever feel so totally overwhelmed about something that you didn't think you could move on? Have you ever gone through a period of time when you thought no one in the world understood you — not even your friends — and sometimes you even hated yourself? Did you ever have to deal with someone in your family getting divorced? Or dying? And what about friends? Is it hard to make friends or keep friends? Are there any relationships in your life that you would like to improve?

These are just a few of the reasons why people consider getting help and they are not necessarily related to any mental illness. They are simply a part of being human.

Remember, Michal, people shouldn't have to struggle with the tough things in life all by themselves.

It is a lot easier to do it with someone else.

Rabbi Hochberg

Dear Rabbi,

My parents have wanted me to go to a shrink for a long time. At first, I used to totally fight them on it, but lately I have been feeling so awful and depressed, I think it is probably a good idea. But here's my question: How do I know what kind of shrink to go to?

Tzvi

Dear Tzvi,

I'm sorry to hear how awful you are feeling and am glad you decided to get help. The good news is that most people who go for help usually get better.

I am assuming you are asking me how to choose a good therapist who practices "talk therapy." Here are a couple of useful guidelines:

1. You need to feel comfortable with him or her. Otherwise you won't be able to get into some of the areas that you really need to work through.

2. The therapist should have some experience in helping people who struggled with the same thing you are struggling with. Don't be afraid to ask if he or she has treated others in similar situations.

3. There is a lot of overlap between spirituality and the human psyche (e.g., feeling guilty and depressed because you did an *aveirah*), so it is important to work with someone who understands both of these areas well. All things considered, if you have a choice between two equally competent therapists, you should choose the *frum* one. He or she can help you professionally while remaining within a Torah framework. If you have to make a choice between a more competent therapist or a more religious one, please consult a halachic authority about what is best for your individual situation.

4. Remember, sometimes it is a good match between you and the therapist and sometimes it isn't. If it is not working, you have to try to find someone else. Don't feel stuck. There are a lot of great therapists out there, so keep looking until you find the one that is best for you.

Good luck, Tzvi.

Rabbi Hochberg

Dear Rabbi,

My friend told me that she often makes herself throw up after lunch by sticking her fingers down her throat. I'm totally freaking out! I'm trying to help her and she made me promise not to tell anyone. What should I do?

Shanah

Dear Shanah,

You know the expression "between a rock and a hard place"? Sound familiar?

But I have to tell you something really, really critical. In fact, it is so critical, that your friend's life may depend on it.

If you are trying to help your struggling friend, remember that although you may be willing to do anything for her, this is completely out of your league. I can't even tell you how many times I've heard, "I'm helping my friend with her eating disorder...I'm like her psychologist...is that okay?" My answer is always the same: No, it is not okay. You are a great friend and you want to help, and the best way to do that is to encourage your friend to get the professional help she needs. Be as convincing as you possibly can. And if she refuses, and you need to tell a teacher or guidance counselor, then take a deep breath and just do it.

Now, you may be thinking, "But how can I betray my friend? She trusted me! What kind of friend am I if I tell on her to the guidance counselor? She'll hate me forever!"

Great question.

Here's the answer...

You are someone who cares so deeply about another girl that you are willing to possibly throw away your friendship in order to get her the help she needs. You are someone who is willing to risk being very uncomfortable, maybe even never talking to this girl again, in order to make sure that she will be okay. You are someone who is willing to endure very unpleasant and awkward situations for another girl's sake because you know that ultimately you are doing what is best for her.

So, Shanah, you tell me:

What kind of friend are you?

Rabbi Hochberg

GLOSSARY

Aharon — Aaron, the high priest

aveirah(os) — sin(s)

Avraham — Abraham

Beis HaMikdash — Holy Temple

beis midrash — Study hall

bashert — Divinely predestined marriage partner

bechirah — Free will or free choice

beis din — Jewish court

berachah — Blessing

bitachon — Trust in G-d

baruch Hashem — Thank G-d

chesed — Kindness

chesed shel emes — True kindness

daven — Pray

emunah — Faith in G-d

frum — Orthodox

Gan Eden — Garden of Eden

Gehinom — Hell

halachic — Relating to Jewish law

halachos — Jewish law

kohen gadol — High priest

Lechah Dodi — Part of the Friday night prayers for the Sabbath

l'sheim Shamayim — For the sake of Heaven (G-d)

maariv — The evening prayer

mechitzah — Physical divider between the genders, usually found in the synagogue

menorah — Holy candelabra that was in the Holy Temple

Middah — Character trait

mikveh — Ritual bath

mitzvah(os) — Commandment(s) in the Torah

Moshe — Moses

neshamah — Soul

Pirkei Avos — Ethics of the Fathers

rabbanim — Rabbis

Rosh HaShanah — The Jewish New Year

rosh yeshivah – Dean of religious Jewish school

Shabbos — Sabbath

shalom bayis — Harmony between husband and wife (literally, "peace in the home")

shemiras negiah — Refraining from physical contact with a member of the opposite gender who is not an immediate family member

Shemoneh Esrei — Prayer said three times daily

shiur — Lecture

shomer negiah — Keeping the prohibition of *shemiras negiah*

shul — Synagogue

simchah — Celebration (e.g., bar mitzvah or wedding)

tefillah — Prayer

Tehillim — Psalms

teshuvah — Repentance

tzenius — Modesty

yeshivah — Religious Jewish school

yetzer hara — Evil inclination or Satan

yichud — Prohibition against being alone with a member of the opposite gender who is not an immediate family member

yiras Shamayim — Fear of Heaven (G-d)

Yom Kippur — The Day of Atonement

zechus — Merit

Zohar — Kabbalistic work attributed to Rabbi Shimon bar Yochai

zt"l — Acronym for "of blessed memory"

INDEX

· · · · · · · · · · ·

ABOUT THE AUTHOR

Rabbi Dovid Hochberg, LCSW-C, is the director of the Maryland Counseling Network. A much sought-after psychotherapist, he is well known for his highly successful work with clients. He has published and lectured extensively on parenting, mental health, and relationship issues and is a widely consulted expert in these areas.

Rabbi Hochberg received his rabbinical ordination from HaRav Shmuel Yaakov Weinberg, *zt"l*, of Ner Israel of Baltimore and his master's of social work from the University of Maryland. He is currently pursuing his doctorate in psychology.